EFFING SIMPLE YOU

YOU DO YOU

BY

Toni Vanschoyck

Effing Simple—a Series

Ordering Information: Quantity sales—special discounts are available on quantity purchases by corporations, associations, U.S trade bookstores, wholesalers, and others. Please contact Toni Vanschoyck at www.effingsimple.com.

www.DreamStartersPublishing.com

Table of Contents

Praise for the first book in the series:

Effing Simple: Your Guide to Growing Your Network Marketing Business and Changing Your Life

She says it all the time! She proves it! Believe it and just do it! — From the first time I met Toni, she said it is really simple. I kept thinking, “no it can't be that simple. There has to be a secret to this success. She must be holding something back!” I went out searching and in the meantime she wrote this book. I have come back around full circle and found...it is EFFING simple! All these other people that you can hire will tell you the same thing in a different way. So save yourself some money and buy this book. Read it. Do what it says and watch yourself soar to the top.

I have purchased several copies of the book. I use it at my events to tell my story about looking elsewhere for the key to the business when all along it was right in front of me with my leader. RIGHT IN FRONT OF ME!

— P Mccoy

Amazing Book for Entrepreneurs. I have gotten great nuggets. It's relatable, motivational and gives you practical tips without unnecessary filling. It makes being an entrepreneur literally "effing simple.”

— Benson

Great book! Wow love this book! Toni is amazing and her no nonsense approach to business is so refreshing! Love the tools she has offered too. Find your why and get out of your head and into business.

— Shawna Inman

Real, easy to follow and great guidance, action steps. I was impressed with how the book is written. More like someone is sitting across from you and speaking to you vs being lectured to with a how to guide approach, as many similar books are structured.

Simply stated, if you like real, then this is the book for you.

— Shirley Zinn

What a Motivational Kick in the Pants! Toni and Jay really tell it how it is in a way that gets you fired up and ready to work harder and put yourself out there more. As soon as I was done reading Effing Simple, my husband read it too! After reading this book I am getting up earlier and working harder with a much better mindset than ever before. I am really enjoying the extra web content that sends the educational journey home after finishing the book. I will be getting this book for all of my new team members and after reading this I know there will be many more!

— Melissa Troulis

Learn from the Best! I have known Toni & Jay for many years and I have watched them build their business from the ground floor up. Toni has a no nonsense approach and practices what she preaches. I loved her chapter on The Drama Ditch. We all need to get rid of the drama and do follow the philosophies of the secret. What we put into our brains is what comes out. Thank you, Toni for paving the way for so many and making it so Effing Simple!

— Tammy Causley

It's that SIMPLE. This book will change your whole perspective on network marketing, and make you a believer. I've personally known Toni going on four years. I've attended many events, heard her speak, and watched her grow as a leader for so many. Toni tells it like it is, without the fluff. I love her and the way she simplifies the process. This book will change your life!!

— Kathy L Claybaugh

Must Read! This book is an absolute must have for anyone working in network marketing. Toni has earned the effing $5M so she obviously knows what she is taking about. From now in I am getting a copy to all my girls joining my team because it will no doubt help them succeed and reach their goals.

— Lana Severinsky

Made me cry ugly tears. This book touched me so deeply that I was brought to tears. Toni tells it like it is and shares how she grew her business. I am implementing her strategies to get out of debt myself. Thank you, Toni and Jay for keeping it #effinsimple.

—Crystal

Life Changing Read. Toni's bold, call it like it is, paint the wall with your excuses then shoot holes in all of them is a refreshing reminder of how to make it in this type of business. If what you are currently doing isn't working, read this then take a fresh look in the mirror and take action, this is your "wake-up call" wish granted.

—MG

Acknowledgements

Of course, this book wouldn't have happened without my family and my network marketing family. Because of them, I was led here.

Thank you to my husband, Jay, the girls, Naomi and Catherine, and of course, our trifecta. Keep reaching for the stars and when you think you have dreamt big, dream bigger!

Please note some of the names have been changed or omitted to protect identity.

Foreword

Hi everyone. My name is Jay Treloar and my wife is that amazing rockstar, Toni Vanschoyck. Toni is one of the most amazing people I've ever met in my life. She, as you may know, has experienced some just incredible success in network marketing, but she's also had to overcome some obstacles as well. In 2014, she found a network marketing company that piqued her curiosity and kind of lit that spark. But, the organization didn't have any information other than an idea at the time she was introduced. They didn't even have a website! Regardless, she went down and met with the owners and the amazing management team of the company to hear what they wanted to do and what was about to come to fruition. That meeting, really, really turned Toni's little spark into an inferno.

Her desire to join the company wasn't met with enthusiasm all around. In fact, most people were not supportive of her joining yet another network marketing company—especially after the last one failed. But one thing's for sure, Toni followed her heart. She knew she had to do, what she was being led to do. In essence, she did what she teaches in this book: Toni did Toni.

Within six short months of starting with that company, Toni was able to retire me. She was able to completely replace my income. And now, here we are five years later, and there are a quarter of a million people that Toni teaches, coaches, trains—internationally, not just here in the United States, but all over the world. And those quarter million network marketers are working on that company's next billion dollars in annual revenue.

After a couple of years on the sidelines, I got the itch to do what Toni was doing. And so now for the past almost three years, she and I have been working on this business together. We have literally traveled the world and have met other network marketing professionals. Our experience with network marketing gave us the platform and the springboard into our idea of creating Effing Simple. Sometimes we all overcomplicate things. Sometimes we just can't get out of our own damn way. The first book in the Effing Simple series was designed for network marketers. It's a simple step by step approach on how to be successful. You can teach, you can coach, you can train, you can help people, but unless you show them the simplicity, sometimes they just don't know how and they can't experience the success they desire. The first book provided the Effing Simple help people need to succeed as a business owner.

And we didn't really realize it at the time, but we were creating a movement—**an Effing Simple movement people have really latched on to**. And in realizing what goes into business, Toni realized that you can't really separate personal and self-development and work. It all kind of goes together. This book, Effing Simple You: You do You, is about how to get out of your own way, how to truly maximize your potential as an individual, how to simplify overwhelming things, and how to create a life of abundance and love. And isn't that really what life is about? Abundance and love, whether it's money or spirituality or whatever it is. That's the key to a happy, healthy, successful life is what you define it as.

And that's what this book is about. I've watched her working on it, I've read it, and it is just going to be the most amazing thing that you've ever read. I'm biased, but you know I'm right. Also, please, please, please keep an eye out in early 2020 for our podcast. We are starting an Effing Simple podcast, weekly chats, videos, things to help foster what we're talking about with the book series. Effing Simple is a movement and we want to reach as many people as possible. We want to help people on their way to abundance and on their way to loving themselves.

Introduction

Marge found herself alone in her home one day. The kids were off to school, her husband at his job in the city, and the dog napping in the yard. For the first time, since the summer, and crazy vacation time with her family, Marge felt like she pressed the pause button. She could actually think, and reflect on where she was in life.

She felt like she had a nice relationship with her husband, but missed the emotional and physical intimacy they once shared. Her kids loved her, and she loved them, but the "mother" role seemed to create a boundary between a pleasant surface relationship, and the type of deeper relationship she yearned for—especially now as her girls were entering middle and high school. Of course, the dog was her usual silly, loyal self, and Marge realized the relationship she had with the dog was probably her most "natural" relationship. No judgments. No expectations beyond being cared for. And, at times, a level of comfort—of just being able to be herself—that Marge missed about the other relationships in her life (including her colleagues).

Marge volunteered for a local philanthropic club, and felt most of her relationships with the other volunteers were strained and temporary. Jill was her only true friend from that group. Marge and Jill shared coffees, shopping trips, and chit chat now and then—but, again, nothing really deep. Jill wasn't a true confidant. They shared a shallow level of trust that, though nobody's fault, seemed to keep things distant.

Bottom line: Marge was uncomfortable in the vast majority of her relationships. It wasn't that she felt unloved—she knew she was loved. At the same time, she knew something was missing. It wasn't anyone's fault, but Marge wondered what she could do to feel differently and have different experiences. She wasn't sure if her concerns were unrealistic expectations about what life and relationships should be like. Nonetheless, she wanted something different. As a successful entrepreneur, Marge helped support her family, pay for vacations, contribute to college funds, and manage the household bills. But, in many ways, Marge felt like a bit of a failure. It was hard to put her finger on it, but the unsettling feeling was undeniable.

Effing Simple You—You do You was written to help people like Marge, and is based on my own philosophy of life. As we all go through struggles, and tackle the demons and difficulties that present themselves, I think some of us forget to let go of those, and figure out a way to move forward in a way that honors who we are, how far we've come, and the incredibly bright potential we have. It's important to continue on our way in life; despite—or maybe because of—any hurdles we've overcome.

I believe there are five simple principles to living a fulfilled life, and each of these principles breaks down past, present, and future barriers that you, Marge, and everyone else will probably face. And, although none of us goes through life in the same way, I've found these principles to be universal, especially in today's economic and cultural environment.

If you know me, you know I won't spend time on "fluff" and "bullshit." This is not a book to read, think about and put away. This is a workbook that will put you through the steps to creating a more fulfilling life by focusing on your relationships; with yourself, with your friends and family, with your career, with your community, and in your world. In this book, we will whittle down the simplest aspects of finding this satisfaction in life; touching on the basics of friends and family, and looking at those. But, not just on the surface. We'll dive deep, and answer the question:

If you don't have productive relationships, why is that?

I'm going to be asking you to look in the mirror, and I mean looking hard in the mirror, at why this question might feel like it's hitting you hard. When I've asked myself that question, at various times in my life, or asked others who are struggling, I find the answer fairly universal. It doesn't matter if

I'm asking a friend, female or male, or a colleague. It doesn't matter if I'm asking a family member who seems to be flailing, or someone who is opening up to me within the realm of my work as a business coach.

Usually, the common struggle comes back to the person putting too much value on what other people say or think. The root of this particular struggle **always** comes down to self-love and self-esteem. No matter what the issue looks like, that's what the underlying issue boils down to.

Throughout this book, I will challenge you to take a very, very close look at how well you know yourself, how much you love yourself, and to what degree you value the opinions of others more than your own. How much do you value someone else's knowledge above your own? How often do you put your own dreams, goals and beloved activities aside, because you feel pressure from someone else? How many people have told you, "You should…?" More importantly, how much value do you put into those questions from others?

The life principles we'll be going through here are not simple "life hacks." There are no shortcuts to finding the level of fulfillment missing in your life. These are principles that, while simple, will take some real backbone to lift up and carry forward as you discover and apply them to your life. Lord knows, we're all different, and come from different backgrounds and experiences, so I can't dictate exactly how you'll integrate these ideas into your life. However, I do believe with consistent effort, you'll find your life can become easier and more fulfilling. When that happens, your relationships—all of them—can improve, in time.

So, buckle up buttercup. Let's cut through the BS and get started with your Effing Simple life! Let's take a quick look at the five man principles we'll be diving into in this book.

The Five Principles/Pillars:

Family
Friends
Finances
Fitness
Faith

Depending on where you are in your life, the above pillars may or may not be in balance. Balancing these aspects leads to a fulfilled life—and I'll show you ways to do just that.

Think back to Marge for just a bit. She had good things going on in most, if not all of these areas. But, were they balanced? How about her relationship with herself? How does that fit into these five pillars? What do we know about her "faith?" (And, no, I don't just mean religious faith here.) How about her health—physical and emotional? Could these be playing into, positively or negatively, her sense of self and well-being? How does Marge balance her relationship with her family and the relationships with her friends? Is she not giving enough time to either, or too much time to one over the other(s)?

We'll bring our story back to Marge in this book, as well as other colleagues and friends I've been honored to work with throughout my own life journey. I don't sit here in judgment of you and your struggles. I've gone through many of them myself, and continue to work on finding and maintaining a happy balance in my life. So, I'll also share stories of when I've triumphed, and when I've blown it...

Listen, I didn't come up with five pillars. Honestly, I don't know where these were first outlined, or by whom. Even with a bit of research, I couldn't uncover the origin of these five pillars. But, when we look at them, with open and honest eyes, I think we can see that these five pillars come from a place of common humanity, and even through some organized faith. But, the bottom line is that we can all relate to them, and we can all take stock on where we are in life when we examine our own lives through the spectacles of these five core principles.

When I first explored these five principles in my life, it really stuck with me. I realized when I excel in all five areas, my life is pretty comfortable. I don't mean "comfortable" in the sense of having a nice car, being able to take amazing vacations with my family, or in the notion of being able to afford a big house. Of course, financial security is a big part of that, but it is **one** aspect of life, and only one.

Your relationship with money, or your relationship with your health, needs to be balanced with every other aspect or principle. Family, Friends, Finances, Fitness, and Faith need to be held to the same degree of importance in your life. If one principle overwhelmingly supersedes the others, your relationships in all aspects of your life will suffer. Most of all, your relationship with yourself and those closest to you will undergo hardship.

Marge is in all of us. We've all had times in our lives when maybe we felt like giving up. Or, maybe things were going well, but there was this inexplicable emptiness in our lives. Wherever you are today, we'll go through things, peeling back layer after layer, to uncover what it is YOU can do to bring balance into your life—even if it's for the first time in your life. We'll tackle some tough questions, but we'll do it in a way that honors wherever you are in your life.

If you know me and my work, you'll know I don't beat around the bush. I may sometimes seem a little "rough around the edges," but know t it's because I don't want you to waste your time or money running circles on the hamster wheel of life. That gets you nowhere, and I think it actually takes you back in your progress. To move forward, you have to stop staring at the ground, look at the bigger picture of where you are in life, and determine how you are affecting everyone around you.

Family is not an important thing. It's everything.

Michael J. Fox

Chapter 1

Family

Let's start with family. They come first, right after you take care of you. I think most of us can agree with that, but let's get one thing clear. Family isn't necessarily restricted to those related to us by blood. Family can be someone you meet along the way, at some miscellaneous point in your life, and you feel like they are your soul-brother, soul-sister, or whatever.

Some of us are blessed with a wonderfully, supportive blood family. However, my experience has shown me that many, if not most of us, have members of our family who are assholes. I know in my own family, there are several individuals I don't even talk to. I have had to let some of these people go, and they are, effectively, out of my life. The ones who I'm thinking of are stuck in negatively, and the "blame game" is alive and well with how they process their own experience in life.

After fifty years of life, I learned when to say "Enough is enough!" I've seen friends of mine experience the same thing with members of their own families. When the mother of one friend was telling her, "You're just lazy, and will never amount to anything," in front of her own child, that was enough. Another friend walked away when her aunt asserted, "Here, make yourself useful," while throwing a pile of disorganized clothing at her—after she spent more than 10 hours helping her aunt unpack from a move to the area.

And, let me tell you—when you walk away from an abusive family member—whether it's physical or emotional abuse, you owe them NO explanation. Their narcissism, which is usually where abusers fall, will keep them from ever understanding or empathizing. In this case, there's no need to waste your time with them anymore. They are not really family. They are merely blood relatives. We're told to respect our parents, but that's bullshit when parents don't respect their children. If a parent or family member doesn't treat you with respect, and in a way that you know you should be treated, then "Bye, Felicia!"

Family, in this context, certainly can be blood relatives, but it can also be people you choose to surround yourself with; people who love and support you unconditionally. I choose to include unconditional supporters in my life. In turn, I make sure to I offer that same love and support to them.

How is your family serving you? Are they constantly putting you down, or are they lifting you up? Are you telling you that you "can't do it," or are they cheering you on? Are they telling you you're not good enough, or reminding you that you can do anything?

I've had family members tell me basically, I was a "piece of shit," or that I "sucked." Now, why on earth would I put up with that? If you are getting that kind of "love" from your family, why ask yourself why you allow it. That goes the same for a significant other and in your relationship with a spouse or life partner. I've been there, too.

Too often, I see my friends and colleagues struggling with their family, and a lack of support from people who SHOULD be supporting them. I think, in part, this is because those family members want my friends and colleagues to settle for mediocrity, like they did. It goes back to a lack of balance that they have in their own lives. They don't have any true self-love, so they bring others down to make themselves feel better. After 50 years of life, I finally understand the saying, "Misery loves company." Often, the people who give you are hard time are threatened by your success, your happiness, and your willingness to fly high above mediocrity. In other words, they are jealous.

I divorced some members of my family long before I became very successful in life. But, I've also had to walk away from blood relatives and "friends" who just can't handle the success. You know you've "made it" in life when you have "Negative Nancys" and haters. They just can't deal with your willingness to risk things to have a better life. They think you are "crazy" because you're doing things differently. There comes a time in life to stop putting up with things that don't serve you.

I had one friend who retired early, at the age of fifty. She and her husband paid down all their debt, purchased two sailboats (one in Mexico for warm water sailing, and the other in southern California for cool summer sailing), purchased a second home in central Mexico, and basically lived their lives happily retired; participating in their community, taking painting lessons, music lessons and getting to know their new communities. One of their relatives was heard telling another, "Maybe we're the crazy ones...maybe those two have it figured out." Damn right, they did!

In light of all this, and in light of what this chapter gets down to—family is everything. Family includes those in your life in the right way—supporting you, cheering you on, and believing in you. Whether blood related or not, they should be one of your priorities. This needs to include your own immediate family. If you have a healthy family relationship with your husband or wife, and your kids (if you have them), then you can realize this part of the equation of finding balance in your life.

A healthy relationship means you can talk to each other, and more importantly, listen to each other. A healthy family relationship is when each of you feels like you can be yourself around each other. A healthy family relationship is when you know you would do anything for the other people in your family, and you know they have your back, too. These people will get up in the middle of the night and bail you out of jail.

Most of us don't have a perfect family; but, maybe that family is perfect for us. Whatever weaknesses or limitations any individual has, maybe it's to help us learn how to balance things out in a way that we couldn't do by ourselves. A friend of mine is married to a wonderful woman. She is very intuitive, thoughtful and grounded. But, one of her limitations is that she tends to worry too much about things she doesn't have control over. Her spouse, on the other hand, is less intuitive about other people, and doesn't worry too much about things. Together, they balance each other out. One helps the other worry less about things, and the other helps their partner learn to read and trust impressions about people in their lives.

The more you develop who you are, and become stronger and more confident in who you are, the more you can choose meaningful relationships, and nurture healthy connections with your family. Again, whether or not your family is blood related isn't as important as understanding your boundaries, and what you will put up with. What can you learn from them? How can you support each other? What is it that you each bring to the family table?

You choose who you have in your life. In many ways, life will hand you what you tolerate. If you only tolerate healthy relationships in your life, that's what life will bring you. If you tolerate crappy relationships and crappy people in your life, that's what you'll get more of. You do take the weather with you, and I'm sure you've seen people who have gotten into toxic relationship after toxic relationship. Until they can develop healthy, happy boundaries with themselves and then with others, this pattern will continue throughout their life.

As you continue on your adventure in life, it's important to consistently evaluate who is in your family circle. Consider, are they supportive, overall? Of course, no one person will back every single thing you do. Maybe they can't support a decision you make here or there. But, if lack of support is a pattern, and you're not getting assistance from them, no matter what you do or try, it's time to eject them from your circle. If, on the other hand, a family member in your life is generally supportive, and even if they don't agree with a decision you make, they respect you and your right to make that decision (even if it turns out to be a mistake), then those are the type of family members you want to keep in your circle.

If there's someone in your life you think you need to let go, or "dis-invite" them from your circle, it's really easy to figure it out. Make a simple list of "Pros" and "Cons" of having them in your life. Seriously. Sit down and make a list to compare the pros and cons. If there are more cons, then you need to really evaluate how they are in your life. As you become more positive in your life, and you stop the negative chatter in your head, and deflect negative chatter from others, you can more easily shed negative people and negative situations.

When I was a little girl, I wanted to be a truck driver. I thought that would be the coolest gig on the planet—traveling across the country, driving a big rig, and being my own boss. When we're little kids we had big dreams like that, right? Well, I was told "No, there aren't lady truck drivers." So often, we're told "No, no, no" throughout our childhood. Not surprisingly, the dream to be a truck driver just faded away for me.

Too often, we shut down the dreams of little girls and boys who want something from life. We think or say, "No, you can't do that…" However, kids who accept these thoughts grow up conditioned to hearing "No," and being ok with that. I'm here to say you shouldn't let anyone tell you "No." REAL family believes in you, no matter how "crazy" your dream might be. Disclaimer, I do NOT mean anything that can cause harm or foul to another.

As you grow and develop, you become less and less tolerant of the negativity. You become less tolerant of people telling you, over and over, what's "wrong" with what you're doing. Because, at that point, you just don't want to hear it anymore. You know what's right for you, and even if it turns out to be a mistake, you know you will learn and grow from that experience.

One of my dear friends has a line I use all the time. It came about when her brother, who didn't own a home, or even a decent car, and basically didn't have a career or job that he liked, nor any meaningful, lasting relationships in his life. He was kind of passing through life—which is fine, if you're happy, but he wasn't. He always judged her, and gave "advice" on what she should do.

One day, when she was choosing how to decorate her house—a home she purchased, on her own, after divorcing just a couple years before, her brother came over. He said to her, as she was picking out colors for her living room, she should paint the heat/air conditioning registers a "flat black." She looked at him, and without blinking said, "Well, when you have your own house, I guess you can paint your registers flat black."

I loved that, because she told him that his idea was ridiculous for her, and also demonstrated firm boundaries. She didn't have to tell him to f*** off in so many words. At the same time, she made it clear she didn't need, want, or would tolerate his unsolicited advice. Since then, she's used that philosophy to deflect "advice" people give her on how she should live her life. She just doesn't tolerate that type of interference.

What should you tolerate? You should tolerate and invite love from your family. You should tolerate and invite positivity and encouragement. When you invest in your self-esteem, and your self-worth and your self-love, and you really start focusing on what YOU want, you tolerate, less and less, from those who are working and acting against you.

When choosing your family, it's important to focus on key things so that you can have this mentality of tolerating only positive, healthy, and balanced relationships. You can walk into a room and read people's energy, especially after you've been working on yourself for so long. You can feel the vibration of the energy that someone is giving off. Are they repelling you? Are they negative? If yes, you can simply walk away. On the other hand, are they inviting and positive? If yes, that's where you want to spend your own energy.

Once you find those people, then you do whatever you can, and need to, to preserve that relationship, and nurture each other. When you find people who take ownership for whatever happens in their life—good or bad—celebrate them as they would celebrate you. When you create your family of people who surround you and cheer you on, through your ups and downs, triumphs and mishaps, without judgment, but only admiration, you have your family. These are the people you protect, the relationships you protect, and the family you create to support and believe in each other. When you are around your family, especially the type of family I'm talking about, your energy increases. So much so that you feel almost invincible. Because you know, in your heart of hearts, they have your back, and you have theirs. There's nothing that beats that feeling. With this principle in place—a healthy, loving, and supportive family (be they blood related or not)—you can accomplish just about anything.

Homework

How do you define family?

Who is in your family?

How do you need to strengthen your family?

What are some action steps that you can commit to, in order to strengthen your family?

A true friend never gets in your way

unless you happen to be going down.

Arnold H. Glasgow

Chapter 2

Friends

When I think about what it all comes down to for me, it's integrity. I think it's my duty to show full integrity to anyone and everyone I meet—especially when it comes to my business adventures. I expect the same from those around me. As I've gotten older, I realize my circle of friends gets smaller, even though the number of my acquaintances continues to grow. I realize that if someone doesn't demonstrate integrity, honesty, and respectful behavior towards me, my family, and the people I care about, they are not going to be in my circle anymore.

I almost feel "integrity" is a love language. What better way to show that you love yourself, and those around you, than live your life with integrity? What better way to demonstrate that you respect yourself and those around you, than live your life with integrity? What better way to build a career, than live with integrity? In my opinion, showing up with integrity is the best way to walk the talk of being a good person and spread love around the world.

As I've honed in on how to live my life with integrity, and model that way of life to those around me, the result is a shrinking circle of friends—and that's okay. But, the circle of friends, though smaller, is stronger than ever, and continues to grow stronger. This filtering of who belongs in my circle doesn't happen overnight. It happens in stages. It's really a process of elimination, where I recognize those who will be a negative drain rather than a positive influence.

What I've seen, and if you've been on a path of positivity for some time, you've probably seen, is that positive attracts positive. Likewise, negative attracts negative. Just the sheer fact that I choose to live life in a positive way attracts others who want to live THEIR lives in a positive way. For example, when faced with a challenge, I typically charge forward. As a mentor once told me, "You either step in a pile of shit and keep walking, or you step around it—either way, you keep moving through that pile. You don't just stand there…"

Do you know people who love to stand in a pile of crap? Usually, to be honest, the pile is of their own making. While standing in it, they choose to feel sorry for themselves, and give up on trying to improve their life. Shitty things happen in life—to all of us. We can either keep walking through that crap, we can plant our feet down firm, or maybe even sit in it, hoping someone will, what, feel sorry for us?

I don't know about you, but crap stinks. I don't want to be around it, and I don't like the smell of it. When someone has been wallowing in negativity, it reeks! And, you can smell it a mile away. Walk, no run, away. There's no reason for you to get covered with their woes. They can carry it themselves.

I've had to let people go, even people who have been in my life for a long time. These are "friends" whose negativity brought me down. Maybe they didn't believe in what I was trying to create for my own life. Maybe they made fun of me behind my back, or to my face, devaluing what I was trying to do. True friends do not do this. They will have a crucial conversation with you over the phone or face to face and that comes from true caring. Some of the friends I released, to be honest with you, were just jealous of the life I created, and were waiting for everything to come crashing down on me. Others would only appear if they needed something from me, but weren't around when I needed them; and sometimes, they are always around lurking but cannot really give anything in return.

In my business, I will go to hell, high water, and back, if I can help. However, there have been some people in the business circle that betrayed my trust and confidence. While I will continue to support them 100% in their business ventures, I had to walk away from them when it comes to the personal side of things.

As you make this change in your life, and filter out so-called "friends" who bring you down, you'll notice improvement in several aspects. You'll probably sleep better. You'll have more money in your bank account. Your relationships with others will probably improve and strengthen. If you're in business for yourself, you'll find it easier and easier to be more and more successful in your business. The weight of someone dragging and slowing you down will be lifted. You may not even have realized how much stress was coming from that one person, or several individuals, until you simply let. them. go.

When you are in a positive state, you literally repel negativity. This naturally happens because negative attracts negative, and positive attracts positive. Likewise, negative repels positive, and positive repels negative. You see it all the time in your relationships, and in how people live their lives. I have a friend from high school who posts on Facebook all the time about one drama after the next "happening" to him. This week, for instance, he is begging his Facebook friends to help him find a new place to live, because of all the "toxicity" he is feeling in his current situation.

Now, if this were a one-off situation, or if I saw this man living life in a positive way, I might reach out my hand to help. But, what I see instead is a man who blames other people, never takes responsibility for his own actions, and is always a victim in his life. It's always “someone did this to me,” or “someone screwed me.” This is a pattern of negativity that attracts further negativity in his life. He’s borderline homeless, has a very low-paying job, is estranged from his daughter and his only grandchild, but he never presses the pause button to see the common denominator in all his pain and hardship. In case it isn’t clear, that common denominator is him.

It’s incredibly sad. Here’s a bright guy, who could still accomplish so much, but he’s buried in his own sadness, anger and negativity. I sincerely hope someday he discovers a way to shift his focus from negative to positive. Even if it’s a small, baby step acknowledging that maybe his anger issues, and recurring substance abuse, is why his daughter doesn’t want him around his grandchild. Maybe one day, he’ll wake up and start taking steps toward shedding the negative around him, including those who are negatively impacting him, and choose a more powerful positive approach to life. Until then, I can’t and won’t help him. He really needs to help himself before anyone could help him. At this stage in his life, if he was offered help, it probably wouldn’t truly help him since it likely would enable more negativity.

With all of this said, I think it's important to be open to the opinion of friends, and even loving, constructive criticism. We can't go around in this world thinking that we're right all the time, and we know the one and only solution for whatever we think our problems are. It would be easy to completely dismiss a friend or family member if they express concern about us. And, even if I said earlier to let go of people who don't support you, I don't want you to think that you should completely dismiss someone if they're expressing a valid concern for you.

If we were to totally disconnect from people who don't agree with us 100% of the time, and share their concerns, we'd be alone in our circle. What's important here is that when concerns are expressed lovingly and sincerely, we should listen lovingly and sincerely. Many of our friends have been through experiences we haven't, and we can always learn from each other. Just like I have advice for people who are trying to build and create balance in their lives, and that comes from my own experience and the experiences of those around me. At some point in your life, someone will express a concern about something that you're doing, or not doing.

Part of finding balance in relationships is being a bit vulnerable, yet strong at the same time. While I don't put up with much BS, there are people in my life whose opinions I value, and who I trust to tell me, lovingly, if they think I'm out of line, or if they think I'm doing something stupid. It would be easy for me to dismiss their concern for me as "judgment," or claim they're just jealous, but this isn't always the case. You don't want to lose people in your life, just because you're stubborn and think you're always right. You're not. No one is. No one is perfect. We all make mistakes, and as long as we learn from them, we can move forward in a great way.

If someone says something to us, and it hits an emotional button particularly hard, that's something we need to look at. Very often, a problem we have with someone else is a problem we have about ourselves. This comes back to self-love, and self-confidence. But, that doesn't mean we should knee-jerk reject any criticism that comes our way. I remember having an argument with my best friend in high school. Of course, I have no idea what we were bickering about, I just remember the moment when my friend said to me, "You're so defensive," and I shot back, "I am not!"

At that moment, I realized the ridiculousness of what I just said. Clearly, I was being defensive. I stopped, looked at her as she looked back at me, and we both burst out laughing. "Well," I said, "maybe a little."

People come into our lives for different reasons. Sometimes it's to help us see something about ourselves that we can't see by ourselves. When that happens, sometimes it gets uncomfortable, and feels downright crappy. But, it's sometimes worth it to take a step back, exhale, look in the mirror, and reflect on yourself and what you're doing. So, while I encourage you to dump the haters, negative people, and people who just don't support you; don't mistake someone having a concern for you as a reason to automatically dump them. They may very well have some wise words that are hard to hear, but can change your life for the better.

The ultimate gift we can receive from friends is when they call us on our bullshit. I call people on their crap all the time in my business. Sometimes, they call me on mine. Here's the bottom line: when we're faced with a situation where we have to fess up to our shortcomings, we have to decide what we're going to do about it. If I call a colleague out on her BS, it's not my responsibility to fix things. It's hers or his. Likewise, when someone calls me out on my stuff, it's MY responsibility to fix it. Period.

When you surround yourself with friends and family members who take responsibility for their words, deeds, and actions, now you've got a strong circle. While you build this circle of friends who are going to help you achieve success in all aspects of your life, don't look for perfection. Like I said earlier, nobody's perfect. You're not perfect. But, if the people in your life, in general, are trying to be good, kind, and hardworking people, then you're golden. The totality of their process is what's important. Keep in mind that there is no perfect person out there for you; either as a family member, a spouse, a friend, or colleague. You may be perfect *together* because they balance your limitations with their strengths, and you balance your strengths with their limitations.

Trying is not doing. It drives me crazy when someone says, "Well, I'll try." Most of the time that's bullshit. You're not going to "try" to call me later, or "try" to finish that project. You either are going to do it, or you're not. But, as long as I see people who are making forward progress, in general, then I love having them in my circle. Likewise, if I start thinking or acting like I'm "trying," then I fully expect someone to call me on that.

The connections we discover and create with friends are sometimes mysterious. You just know when you meet them that you'll be in each other's lives in a very meaningful way. I met a young girl recently. Chloe is in her twenties, and just moved to our area. She has a young baby, and doesn't know a soul. But, I just immediately connected with her. We have virtually nothing in common. I have kids her age! But, there was something that drew her to me, and drew me to her. Sometimes you just know.

Homework

How do you define friendship?

___

___

___

Who are your most valued friends in your life?

___

___

___

In what ways do you need to strengthen your relationships with your friends?

___

___

___

Financial peace isn't the acquisition of stuff. It's learning to live on less than you make, so you can give money back and have money to invest. You can't win until you do this.

Dave Ramsey

Chapter 3

Finances

People have such a shitty relationship with money. First of all, they don't understand that money is energy, and I think they put way too much value on money and what the almighty dollar can do. At the end of the day, is it really an almighty dollar? What does money represent in your life? Does it represent how much crap you can buy? Does it represent where you can go on vacation? Does it represent which type of college you can send your kids to? Does it represent your financial worth and value in the community?

The amount of money you make is equivalent to how much you value yourself. And, guess what? We're not taught that. From birth, most of us are taught that money is what you earn so you can acquire things. We're taught to live to work, not work to live. We're trained to enslave ourselves to the pursuit of the almighty dollar—happiness be damned.

My father was the first person who taught me that our relationship with money needs to be a little different. He made it clear that it wasn't good enough to have a job that we hated, even if the money was good. I remember him telling me, "I just love working." He showed me how important it is to love what you do, and to make sure to have multiple streams of income.

While my dad was very successful at making money, and we didn't have a great relationship for a long time. Because I was too young and naive to know otherwise, I framed the money he made, and his success in the corporate world, as a negative thing. To me, for many, many years, money was an asshole. Because my dad made a lot of money, I felt money made him an asshole—which is completely not true. You can obviously be an asshole without any money.

One thing that I knew without a doubt was that my reflection on money a long time ago was very blue collar. I was trading time for money. I wasn't making money work for me. The restaurant jobs I had demonstrated this. I started bussing tables when I was sixteen. I had a really good work ethic. I would go in on Friday afternoon, (because I couldn't work during the school week), and I'd work open to close on

Saturday, and all day on Sunday. I got my 30 hours in—just during the weekend.

I did this until the time I graduated high school. After that, I was working two jobs and going to college part time. I always paid my own bills, though my dad helped me out with college. I knew how to balance a checking account. I knew where my money went, and I worked hard for it. This is something I think we should teach our kids. I think teaching them about money is way more valuable than throwing money at them to get a college degree that may not even help them get ahead. Teaching our kids to have a healthy relationship with money should be a priority, versus paying their way to acquire a piece of paper that may be worthless, unless they're pursuing a career that absolutely requires that piece of paper.

In our society, we're all taught to do this. We are told to trade our time for money. Maybe that made sense fifty years ago, but that's not working for us anymore. You have to master your own self-education when it comes to money, and understand how to make it work for you. Here's where my dad nailed it. First things first, you have to do something you love. The one thing that I know, and all the people I know who have been successful, is that if they're not operating in the space of doing something they love, they're never going to become prosperous.

We were meant, and were put on this earth, with one unique skill set, and when we do something that we love, that's how we become financially independent. What that is, and what that looks like, is going to be different for everybody. Only you know, in your heart what you love, and how you can turn that into financial independence and prosperity. Go back to those dreams you had as a kid. What fuels your fire? I don't care what it is; maybe you just want to knit for the rest of your life. Maybe you want to open mission centers across the world—maybe that's your passion—maybe that's your calling. You have to follow your calling.

My husband balances me out here, especially when it comes to budgeting, and learning how to stay within a budget. So, I'd like to add his perspective on this here:

One of the things we're taught from day one is to get into debt. "Establish credit," is how we disguise that. "Get a credit card so that you can establish a credit rating." That's what we're taught! But, if you can't afford to buy something, and you "have" to get a loan, then you have no business buying that! If you don't have the money, don't buy it. If you don't have the money, stop going to Starbucks for your coffee five days a week. Stop going out to eat. Stop eating fast food. Make your own meals. You can buy fresh, organic food for a fraction of the price of eating out.

The whole point of finances and financial health is to master your money like you master your mind. You have to make your money go to work for you, and that means multiple streams of income. On average, a millionaire has seven different streams. One needs to be a residual income stream; I don't care what it is. It can be network marketing, dividends paid on stocks, or rental properties.

From there, you can look into investments, flipping homes, building a rental portfolio, or partnering with someone in another business. But, the capital has to come from somewhere, so you have to be saving what you're bringing in, in order to start on this path. You can't invest in real estate, if you have no equity to bring into the market. If you're "investing" by getting into debt, you're just fooling yourself. You have to save and create capital so that you can start this process. It takes just one property, for example, to begin building a rental empire.

You will never get rich working for someone else. Why? Because they're paying you just enough to get by. They're paying you less than you're worth to their bottom line, because you, as an employee, are part of their profit and loss statement. You are in the "loss" column when you work for someone else. They will pay you the least amount they can to make sure that their "profit" line is bigger than their "loss" line in the balance sheet.

There is a certain art to entrepreneurship, and it can be tricky to sort out. This is why network marketing, which is a franchise in disguise, can be a great way to build your own wealth. Everything has been done for you. You don't have to reinvent the wheel when it comes to the product or service, or how to market things. Especially if you establish yourself with a professional corporation, you can literally just run with the materials and resources they have proven to be tried and true. Fill in the blanks with your name, and your twist on what they've already created, since most of the really hard work has been done for you. It's a plug and play model. Plug into what's already been created and structured, and play with your newfound entrepreneurship. The very nature of network marketing means it is highly dependent on providing service to others. In this business, I know I am creating prosperity, in service to others. I get the privilege and honor of helping other people become successful, depending on what success means to them since that's different for everybody.

You can be an employee. You can build your own business from scratch. Or, you can be an independent entrepreneur and take advantage of network marketing opportunities. I've done all three, and have experience in all three ways of making money, beyond residual income like investments (which I'll talk about in a minute). I've always been a hard worker. When I was an employee, I was told when to be at work, how much I could make, and what I could wear to work. And, I did ok. But, then I wanted more, so I started my own small businesses.

Even as a business owner, I was only trading time for money. If our doors weren't open, we didn't have revenue coming in. We were cutting lawns, planting flowers, weeding, and getting paid for that time and effort, and for the time and effort of our employees. If that wasn't happening, live at that moment in time, we made zero money. Plus, we were spending money 24/7, when you consider the overhead necessary to run a business like that. It was really hard to get ahead with such large expenses and limited schedules.

With network marketing, and a consumable product, you can still make money even if you're not doing anything directly related to that effort. As I sit and write this book, I am making residual money from network marketing. I make money while I sleep. You can also utilize e-commerce and social media to earn income. Anyone at any time can go to my website, twenty-four hours a day, and I make money. This is money I earn passively and effortlessly. Then, I can turn that income into even more residual income, via investments, for example.

As far as investing, you can do the same thing here, too. There are financial geniuses out there, like Warren Buffet and other gurus, who have done the hard work for you. They will tell you which stocks to invest in, and when you should transition from volatile stock futures to more conservative investments as you get older (and wiser). You don't have to do all that research. That's just wasting your time. Find an investor philosophy that you believe in, and yes do some basic research, but you don't have to torture yourself finding the "perfect" investment to get started. Be smart, get educated, but know that there are people who have done that work already. You can start making residual income off of your investments, immediately.

One of my financial advisers suggested a couple of stocks for me to invest in a few years ago. Right now, the value of that investment has grown by 5,000%. Who doesn't love that? Make your money work for you, and connect with financial advisors who know what they're doing. Ask around with people you know who are investing successfully, and connect with their consultants.

We have been told throughout our lives that "money doesn't grow on trees," or "you can't afford that." This creates a terrible relationship with money, because that's bullshit. You have to change the message you send to yourself about money, and shift it so it's more positive and productive for you. The wording you use around money, well around anything, is really important. Every time you say something like "I can't" or "I shouldn't" spend money on something, it sends a message that contributes to an unhealthy way of looking at, making, and spending money.

Instead of "I can't afford it," how about, "How can I afford it?" You deserve nice things. Money does grow on trees—maybe not literally, but definitely money can come from "nothing." Instead of thinking or saying, "I can't afford that right now," think, "I choose not to buy that right now, because first I have to do [xxx]." It's not an "I can't" statement, but a "I will do that by doing [xxx]." You have to act like it has already happened—its key to manifestation.

You are worthy, and you deserve whatever you desire in life. Changing what you say to yourself in your head will rock your world. If you always talk about being poor, you're always going to be poor. If you say you can, you can. If you say you can't... guess what? You can't. It's the law of the Universe.

Earlier in this chapter, I said "money is energy." There's a thought that people who are rich are only rich because they scammed people out of money. You'll be poor for the rest of your life if you believe the only way to make a lot of money is by effectively "stealing" it from others. In truth, people can make a lot of money, while providing a lot of value to a lot of people—and I'm a prime example of that.

People who have achieved wealth—and what I mean by the word "wealth" is that their five pillars of life, that we're discussing in this book, are absolutely overflowing. It doesn't necessarily mean money. Prosperity means all of these things. Wealth is represented in what we're talking about: family, friends, finances, fitness and faith. In that frame of mind, having money is only one-fifth of your life. When you have balanced the money part of your life with the other four pillars, that's what truly makes the fundamental difference in being wealthy and prosperous.

Wealth also comes from within, and how you feel about who you are and what you do. For example, there was a two-year gap between two network marketing positions I had. During that time, I still coached and mentored for free. I just loved sharing my passion for making money and helping others live their dreams through network marketing. I was able to align my activities with my values and a sense of community created through my work in network marketing. And, this is because I love what I do, and that's what's the most critical.

In network marketing, for example, you have to love the product, the company, and you have to love the owners. You have to believe in what they have created, and you have to believe in every single one of the people in your network marketing family. When you have this type of love for what you do, that true wealth comes in and works its magic in all aspects of your life. The wealth of spirit you feel then translates into wealth that you can see in your bank accounts.

If you don't have this in place—this love for what you do, what you're selling or working with, and for the people you work with and for—you'll always be desperate. You'll also never be able to balance the four other pillars in your life. You really have to work on them all, each of the five pillars, at one time. If you are really lacking in the finances part of your life, the rest of your life can never be truly fulfilled. Likewise, if you're making a million dollars a year, but you are unhappy in your family and/or friend relationships, you are a very "poor" person, for sure.

I know you've heard the saying, "money doesn't buy happiness," and that's true. That's what I'm talking about here. With all the money in the world, but without balance in the other areas of your life, you can't truly be happy. With that said, money does make life easier. When this has been studied, it's been shown that in today's dollars, a threshold of at least $75,000/year makes people feel their life is much easier than when they are making less than that amount. Does it buy happiness? No, but it makes it easier to feel balance in this area of your life when you're making enough to feel like you can relax around money, and enjoy your life without worrying about your finances.

A final aspect of wealth I want to touch on is the act of giving more as you receive more. When you have achieved that financial balance, giving to others in need, and helping others out, can help balance the overall notion of "wealth" in your life. I once knew a highly successful corporate executive who had come from very, VERY modest roots in rural western Canada. Every day, he would receive donation requests in the mail, and he would sit down at his computer, do a little research to make sure the organizations were legitimate, and write a check, or two, or three. Every day!

I remember asking him why he did that. He told me that when he was a kid, his family came into very tough times. They made it through because of social service agencies and organizations, as well as with community support. He told me, "I never forgot that. I wouldn't be where I am without their help. Now that I can give back, I do."

Feeling connection to your community, and being able to contribute in a way that provides services for people in need, or whatever your passion, infinitely increases your notion of wealth and feeling like you're doing something that really matters in life. What good is your money, especially when you're well beyond that $75,000/year threshold I mentioned earlier, if you are not sharing that wealth with others around you?

Another friend who recently retired, and has disposable retirement income, regularly donates to organizations that provide services for battered women, as well as services that provide low or no-cost health care for rescued animals.

How do you build your own personal wealth to achieve this level of giving? This always, always comes back to how you get your mind around balancing these pillars in your life. And, until you do that, you'll always be flailing. I can honestly say that I didn't have any of this figured out until I was at least 44 years old.

We were doing "ok," but we had little to no savings, we had a few miniscule investments, and when I was out of work for two years, we went through all resources, and…we were in debt. I definitely didn't have my financial pillar balanced out with the rest of my life, and the rest of my pillars suffered, including family, friends, faith, and fitness. This is a mind-shift. You've heard of "mind-fucks," well, this work is a mind-*shift*.

When I finally wrapped my head around this concept and the need to create and balance financial wealth, everything else fell into place. Our net worth is higher than I ever dreamed. Because we have no debt, we feel the comfort of true financial security. My network marketing team sales have totaled **$1 billion** this year. The expansion we're experiencing with a global introduction of the product will only add to that security. But, I'm not here to brag about my "numbers."

I'm here to tell you again and again, no matter how many times you need to hear it, that none of this is possible if you don't have a healthy relationship with money and finances. Not just that you're capable of achieving this type of financial wealth, but that you feel like you **deserve** it. You have to equate having extra money in your life with something you've earned and something you are entitled to. In turn, you have to balance that with the rest of the pillars in your life, and make sure you are sharing that wealth whenever and however you can; whether it's writing checks like my two friends mentioned above, or donating time helping others achieve what you have. It doesn't matter. Keep in mind though, you can't "save" your way to financial freedom. You really have to institute this mind-shift of deservedness coupled with giving.

Balancing the financial pillar in your life isn't about acquiring money solely. Of course, that's part of it—but, the rest is about you and what you do with that money and how you see it and what your relationship to money is. Is it a healthy relationship? Or, are you laden with guilt—or worse, greed?

My network marketing family right now is 200,000 individuals strong. I'd like to see that be up to 1,000,000 people in two years. If I can help 1,000,000 achieve financial independence, that will help me achieve my own sense of financial balance. Wealth is not just about me, and what I accomplish by depositing money in my bank account, or going on vacation with my family. It's about helping 1,000,000 people achieve that same sense of financial security and balance in their life. The CEO I partnered with planted that seed.

I love seeing people take their wealth, and by that I mean emotional as well as financial wealth, to help others in need. One of the organizations that I'm extremely passionate about is Compassion International. My passion was ignited by one person—my friend, Jess. She was the catalyst. Just one person started a movement and I had to be a part of it. This organization has been around for decades, helping impoverished children around the world. Our work through a network marketing company funded, at the writing of this book, more than $340,000, to build and staff four compassion community centers and churches to serve people who don't have enough to eat, maybe live in a cardboard house, and have no access to running water. The centers are located in Columbia, near the border of Venezuela where there are thousands of refugees fleeing the oppressive government and civil war brewing for more than a decade now.

To be able to funnel money and efforts to help refugees is incredibly important to me, and provides a way for me to balance the financial aspect of wealth with the spiritual and emotional aspect of wealth. So, as you build your wealth, in every way possible, I can't emphasize enough how critical it is to recognize how your wealth can help others. Being "rich" isn't about big houses and fancy cars, expensive and numerous vacations. It's about making your world a better place. Yes, your private world, but also your place in the world, and helping those who could use a hand-up. Please invest in T. Harv Eker's book, *The Secrets of The Millionaire Mind* for more inspiration.

Truly giving back can be done on a local basis, too. Find a way to share your wealth. You share wealth every single time you give your time. You share wealth every single time you donate money or knowledge. You share wealth every single time you donate things from your house to a domestic violence shelter, or an orphanage, whether it is near or far, sharing wealth is the true nature of why we are put on this earth. We weren't put here to collect "things." We're supposed to give ourselves away to others in a way that enriches our own hearts, as well as the hearts and lives of those we can help.

Savings is also very important. We have to invest everyday into not just ourselves but our future. Part of being responsible is putting away a portion of what you earn. You need to sit down with a financial planner that has your best interest in mind to create a plan. It is all about you and your future.

Homework

Describe your current financial condition—be honest with yourself—good and bad:

____

____

____

Where do you want to be financially in one year?

____

____

____

Three years?

____

____

____

Five years?

____

____

____

What are some action steps you take toward achieving some of your financial goals?

____

____

____

____

____

____

____

____

____

____

A man of courage is also full of faith.

Marcus Tullius

Chapter 4

Faith

Using your company/business to "minister" the greater good—locally and globally—by using your money and time for a purpose is an important lesson I've learned over time. Now, I'm not talking about "ministry" in the literal sense, as in religious faith, karma, or whatever you want to call it. I'm talking here about using your voice, your company, and your money to minister the greater good to those in your circle, and to the greater society.

When you connect your actions to a bigger purpose, I think you try harder, you think bigger, and your life becomes bigger and more influential than the sum of its parts. And, this begins with you. You can create a collective movement, within your own circle of influence. For example, in regards to the Columbian community centers, people up and down the line of position in our organization have donated. This includes contributions from the president to me, from the founder and people within my own personal family. We've created a drive and a force to bring out the greater good in our community and beyond. Because of these efforts, we get to sponsor 600 children who need our help. These kids get more opportunities, more education, and they're able to improve their lives and their family life.

How does that lead into a discussion about faith, and balancing that aspect of our lives? Connecting yourself to people, and surrounding yourself with people who can see beyond their own lives, and the lives of those around them, is a critical aspect of wealth in the sense of balancing family, friends, finances, fitness, and faith. Sometimes this is because we need to surround ourselves with people who are better at things than we are. Since most people are inclined or drawn to think only inwardly, we need people who can help us lift our eyes and hearts outwardly.

Faith, in this balance, again is not limited to religion—although that can be part of it (if you choose). Religion comes in all shapes and sizes. Beliefs come in all shapes and sizes. I truly don't believe you need a "place" to worship every single time you want to call up to a higher place or presence in your life. Whatever your faith may be; maybe it's the Universe, or maybe it's a specific organized religion or denomination. Whatever your faith is, embrace that. You own that.

The bottom line is, don't be a hypocrite. If you think you're a person of faith, but you're an asshole, then that's a problem. You're being a hypocrite. In *The Code of the Extraordinary Mind*, author Vishen Lakhiani says (I'm summarizing) that we, or most of us, are raised under a specific faith model or organized religion. Who says the way you were raised was the "right way?" For example, there may be things you believe that specific religions advise against.

You get to make your own way in adulthood, and that means, for example, if you grew up in a Christian home, but also believe in certain aspects of Buddhism, own that and embrace that. It doesn't have to be all or nothing. At the end of the day, I truly and firmly feel that faith and what society preaches sometimes falls on the deaf ears of common sense. In some ways, "faith" has replaced common sense, which in many ways has left our society. Why should you preach or teach something, within an organized system of faith, if you don't fully believe it, or think that it's not relevant in today's world?

Faith is a tricky, sticky subject at times—I know. What I'm trying to get at here is effing simple. To help balance faith with the rest of your life, it's important to apply common sense to whatever you believe. Faith means a belief without question. Here's my thought: Simply believing everything without question can be a detriment to full development to sense and think above and beyond yourself and this moment in time. It can be a real stumbling block when it comes to helping others in need, because you might become judgmental and think you're responsible to decide who needs help—and who doesn't—based on your notion or conception of what is "right" when it comes to religion, or a strict definition of faith.

Does a particular religion or system of faith go against who you truly are as a person? Does it cause guilt and pain to conceive or believe certain aspects of your faith? If yes, how does that help you become the best person you can be, and give in as many ways as you can? Does guilt and pain help you find balance between what you believe and your degree of wealth when it comes to your family, friends, and your financial security? Some religions thrive on the notion of creating feelings of guilt. But, why should any religion guilt you into anything?

I honestly think a lot of religion is overrated. If you're living a good life, and you're a good person, at the end of the day, you probably know right from wrong. There are thousands of different faiths in the world. Who am I to tell you what to believe? It doesn't matter to me, as long as you're not a hypocrite, you do the right thing, you are a good person, and you think above and beyond your own personal and immediate needs.

People change over time. What we believe when we're twelve may not be what we believe when we're 18 years old. Likewise, what we believe when we're 18 may not be what we believe when we're 25, 40, or 50 years old. Your life when you're 18 is probably completely different than your life now. Especially for those of you like me who've lived a few decades past that age. I know when I was much younger, my perspective on the world and my role in it was very different than it is now. That's because we all change. Or, at least we should change and evolve, as we collect different life experiences, meet different people, and have our belief systems challenged by the reality we create and the circumstances that happen around us.

I think it's important to re-evaluate every aspect of your life, every six months. This includes the "unquestionables" like your faith. These days, life moves at lightning speeds. How often have you found yourself saying, "Jeez, I can't believe it's already (name a month or year)?" When you're busy, involved, and thinking outside of yourself, time literally flies. If you're not looking in the mirror and inward on a regular basis, I think you're going to miss out on new aspects and depths of life that can really add to the notion of faith and belief. If your life isn't jiving with YOU, then don't do it. Only by stopping, taking a breath, and looking at things do you get to the place where your life and your beliefs match. Then, you stop in a few months, breathe, look and reflect again. Check in with yourself. Are you being true to **your** beliefs about yourself, about your faith, about your community, and your world?

You create more angst, stress, and sleepless nights by doing what you think society is telling you to do—or organized faith may be preaching to you. You know in your heart what you need to do. You know in your heart what is right or wrong. There is very little gray when it comes down to right and wrong, and you know it. Is it better for you **and** the common good? Then, that's the right thing to do. If it's only better only for you nothing outside of you, then, it's probably not the right thing to do. It really is that effing simple. The only way to identify if you are living in that realm of faith is to look, and look deeply at how you're living your life, and see how your life is affecting those around you.

The immense success that happened in my life, and this is my faith, could not have happened without some sort of deity; (without guilt) without some sort of bigger energy force that's moving us all. You can choose to call it whatever you want. Some people call that deity God. Some choose to call it the Universe, or Karma, or Buddha. That doesn't matter to me. But, there are things that will align themselves to you, when you open your heart and you open your mind. Likewise,

I think wonderful things close themselves off to you if don't open your heart, your mind and your spirit. In my book, the notion of faith is not about an organized system of faith or religion. I really think faith is about keeping your eyes, mind, heart, and spirit open to the entirety of the potential your life has to give to and receive from this world.

I believe these bigger, grander forces move for us when we start moving toward greater ideas and thoughts. As you elevate your thoughts and actions, more and more doors will open for you. Maybe it's because you just have more confidence, but I also think there is energy that moves us toward the things we desire, and away from things that don't move us forward. Remember, like attracts like. You have to start putting ideas, thoughts, and feelings out there to start moving in that direction. You must have the balls to put things out there for things to start working and moving with you, toward you, and for you.

In many ways, this discussion is about faith in yourself. If you have faith in your decision-making abilities, and faith in living your life for a greater, grander purpose, this becomes evident in what life brings to you. Self-belief, self-confidence, and self-esteem issues hold people back all the time. I see this everywhere—not just in my organization, but in family and friends, near and far. I think it's the number one struggle people have. If they don't have faith in themselves, the people in their circle, and in their support or lifeline, they will flounder and eventually fail. Sadly, this won't be just personal failure, either. By lacking self-confidence, they can also fail the people who rely on them—even people who don't even know they exist. Our reach in the world goes far beyond people we know immediately. If we've influenced someone significantly, either for good or bad, that person will influence others based on our hold on them. It's our responsibility to believe in ourselves, and have confidence in our living toward a greater purpose, to have a greater positive influence on others. When you apply faith, what is your body saying to you? And I mean faith in everything you do from your health, to your work, to your relationships. Your body will resonate your truth.

Faith starts—and sometimes ends—with you. It starts with reading and thinking positive things and living your mantras every day. It all starts with you having faith in yourself, and those around you, by living your faith. If you start with yourself, you can get where you need to be. I have daily habits that help me stay focused on this, especially if I'm falling short, or feeling tired, or feeling like I need a little boost.

My morning routine is really simple and it helps me get into this way of thinking. We'll cover this routine in detail in Chapter 10. For now, here's an overview. I start off by getting up early, have a glass of celery juice, read something related to personal and/or professional development, have my cup of coffee, and go to the gym. This is my morning five or six days a week, and I think it's a way I can get my head and heart wrapped around the notion of faith.

Whatever you think the Universe might be telling you to do, believe, say, or act on, it has to come first from your heart. This is your core. The Universe starts within, and that's where you must begin. Look at all the external forces in your life. For example, we're taught to believe in specific thoughts, actions, and deeds. Outside forces are always telling us what we should think. That's bullshit! What we should think and believe doesn't start, end, or finish from anything outside of ourselves. If we're being honest with ourselves, all our beliefs and actions come from within.

What do YOU think? What's coming from within? What resonates with you? What echoes from you? The answers to these questions are where you begin to commit to your dreams. You can't quit. These days, it's too easy to do that. We are a culture of instant gratification and lack the balls to stick to and follow through with actions to make our dreams come true. When you let others take your dreams away, you are giving away your power. Spend some time thinking about what you really want and who you want to be. Whatever it is, own that dream. (I've designed a journal to help you with that if you're not sure. Order here: bit.ly/TVEffingSimpleChange.)

I didn't believe in God for a long time. I was, if not atheist, agnostic for sure. I think that was part of my self-limiting beliefs. I could not rectify that there was a higher power, whatever you want to call that higher power. I went to church on occasion when I was a kid. But, I was never required to go. I think I'm kind of grateful for that, because it helped me develop my own belief system, instead of just echoing the belief system of those around me.

I'll tell you what though, everything that's happened in my life certainly wouldn't have happened without the impact of something larger than me. I can't name it, and I can't always explain it. Nonetheless, I know it to be true, and in a very real way. That knowing is a big part of my personal faith and belief system. I see it happen all the time in my life—mountains moving by starting something small or modest, and a higher force helping it evolve and multiply to help more and more people. For example, again, the community centers in Columbia. We started with just one, then two, then three, now four centers were funded in just two months. Who's to even guess what can happen as we focus our efforts, and have them multiplied by a higher power, for four months, 12 months, four years, and beyond?

Faith isn't about me and my individual efforts. It's this power beyond me, and this force of people working, unified, toward a greater good—a common good. This force is inexplicable, sometimes. I think some people need to put a name on it, like God or Karma, or whatever. That doesn't matter to me as much as the results of that force, and how we can create it, multiply it, and increase its positive influence on ourselves, on those we love, those we don't even know, and our community and world at-large.

In my early forties, I went through some really crappy times. In some ways, I think I was being tested to see what I was really made of. There have been times when I didn't feel this sense of faith—in myself, in my loved ones, in my world, and in society. In so many ways now, looking back, I see I was being prepared for bigger, better things in my life, and ways I could positively affect others. A sense of balance in my faith was non-existent then. It was like I was missing a leg, and I was off balance. Sure, I was able to stand up. But I was wobbling and unsteady. Now, with that leg of faith, I can walk, run, and skip to greater and greater things to accomplish in my life, and in the world.

Sometimes when you lose something, or someone you love, it rips your heart out. But, with perspective, wisdom, and experience, the loss allows you to see something much more important later in life. It allows you to see a piece you maybe were missing. Or, maybe it allows you to feel and be vulnerable. Or, maybe it allows you to understand more about your place in the world, and the true notion of living and giving. You can pull from your experiences, and share with other people. When you do this, they can draw strength from you. That's what happens when we go through hardships in our lives. We just don't see it at the moment tragedy strikes. However, trusting and having faith in hardships and our ability to learn from life, is perhaps the best use of faith I can think of.

Flexing our personal faith can create faith in others they may never have seen or believed. Maybe you're the right messenger at the right time, just like others around you have been the right messenger at the right time for you. What better gift can we give ourselves, and others, than being open to messages that ignite us to live our fullest and best life?

That's faith to me. Plus, the ten commandments are the best source of common sense.

Homework

How do you define faith in your life?

____

____

____

Do you feel your faith is balanced with the rest of your life? Why or why not?

____

____

____

What are some action steps you can take to help balance faith in your life?

____

____

____

Exercise is king. Nutrition is queen.

Put them together and you've got a kingdom.

Jack LaLanne

Chapter 5

Fitness

My family used to own a gym. Year after year, especially after the New Year, we'd see people coming into the gym, all gung-ho to get fit, and fulfill their New Year's Resolution. Most would quit after two weeks. Some would last at most, a month. I'm sorry, but I used to laugh at them. They had abused their body for thirty years. To think a month was going to fix everything is laughable.

Fitness can come in many different forms. But, you've gotta do something to get your ass moving at least twenty minutes a day. I don't care what it is. I'm not a size zero. I'm not a size two. But, I live for exercising, practicing yoga, getting into the gym, sweating in a sauna, and taking care of me. This is part of self which I'll talk about later on in this book, but fitness in particular is something that MUST be in balance if you are to achieve true happiness and fulfillment in life.

It's a cliché, but it's true. "You have nothing if you don't have your health." If you've ever had a chronic illness or cared for someone who did, you understand this like no one else can. Maybe you've seen people around you in this position. I'm fifty years old as I write this. I know so many people who are my age, or younger, who can't walk up a flight of stairs without getting seriously out of breath, or who can't see their own feet. I know people younger than me who couldn't get up off the floor if they found themselves on the ground for some reason. That's ridiculous, and there's no excuse for that. If you're an overall able-bodied person, you should be doing everything you can to be as physically fit as you can.

We're just not as active as we used to be. Unless you live in an area of the country where you can walk to go to work, or walk to get your groceries and run your errands, you have to do something specific in the exercise realm. Most of us don't live in a place like that. We drive everywhere, and we've become, frankly, lazy. So, since we drive everywhere, we are effectively sitting on our asses most of the day. Our bodies are designed to move. If they don't move enough, we literally become stagnant and stiff. Our body doesn't function as well, and we get sicker, and sicker, and sicker.

When we take care of ourselves, it helps us with our stress, too. We release endorphins, which are happy hormones that help us stay positive and motivated in life. When we are still, those endorphins aren't being produced, and we slow down even more. When we don't move enough, and aren't eating well, we get fat, because our blood sugar levels are screwed up. In the United States, more than 100 million people are living with pre-diabetes or diabetes (type 2).[1] And, guess what? This is a disease that is 100% preventable, and also reversible if caught early enough. On top of that (and a contributing factor), nearly 40% of US adults are classified as obese.[2]

To gain fitness, we have to start with our consumption regimen, and make sure we're consuming a good balance of food that is fresh, and loaded with essential vitamins, minerals, and healthy fats. I'm not a nutritionist, so I won't go into that here, except to say stay away from any fad diets. What's been proven to work, over and over, and very well researched for decades is a modified Mediterranean diet, with low consumption of simple carbohydrates like breads, sugars, alcohol, etc. I eat clean and organic. I tend to avoid dairy, although I do love cheese. But, cheese can be very inflammatory and it's usually highly processed so it's not great. Anything that comes out of a box or bag isn't really food, at that point. Consume processed foods sparingly.

Exercise alone can't counteract how you eat. If you're eating crap, and exercising like a crazy person, it won't matter. You'll still be at risk of getting very sick—way before your time. With that said, exercise is as important as nutrition. So, you have to find something you love to do, and maybe not think of it as exercise. Think of it as simply moving and doing as much as you can to MOVE more than you typically do in a day. That might mean walking to do a chore, or parking as far away as you possibly can from a store. I don't mean in the parking lot, I mean if your grocery store is five miles away, park ½ a mile away. That's just a 30-minute walk. Gradually increase that distance, or other challenges so you're MOVING EVERY SINGLE DAY!

When you work out, a few things happen to you. Most of us know the cardiovascular benefits, but exercise also helps with your brain health and your emotional health. This is something that fascinates me, so I'm going to do a deep dive here and share with you some of the benefits exercise has on your brain and its ability to solve problems and balance other functions in your body besides just your muscles, heart, and lungs.

First off, when you exercise, your blood flow increases. We all know this. You can feel it in your muscles, and your heart rate increases. With increased blood flow, your brain cells start functioning at a much higher level than when you're sedentary because they're getting more oxygen and more nutrition. You tend to be more alert and awake, as well as focused during and after a workout. I have some of my best ideas when I am working out!

As you build the habit of exercising regularly, at least three to four times a week, your brain gets used to this extra nutrition, oxygen, and exercise. This boosts your brain's ability to function, and protect you from brain related diseases like strokes, Parkinson's disease, and Alzheimer's/dementia. Exercise slows down the aging of your brain and improves its function in the body.

When you exercise, you trigger an increase in neurotransmitters like endorphins, dopamine, and GABA (ok, I had to break open the scientific jargon with this one. GABA stands for gamma-aminobutyric acid. Say that ten times fast—hell, say it once!). The importance of GABA is hard to overemphasize. It actually slows things down so signals don't get crossed, and your body is operating smoothly and in a controlled way.

Finally, in the hippocampus of your brain, as well as in your pituitary gland, exercise is benefiting and balancing how things are working. For example, the hippocampus is the part of your brain where most of your learning and memory are happening. It's also the only part of your brain that can generate new brain cells. When you exercise, you are literally making this happen because of the extra blood flow, nutrition, and oxygen. You get smarter by exercising!

In the pituitary gland, or your brain's control center, exercise helps balance your body's ability to store muscle instead of fat. The pituitary gland releases growth hormone, keeping your body stocked up on muscle, and telling your body to burn fat instead of muscle.

Ok, I've put the textbook down! But, this is some really cool stuff, and I think it speaks to finding that balance in your life. Exercising isn't just about "getting fit." It's about being as smart, and active as you can. It's about slowing down the aging process, and avoiding horrible diseases like Alzheimer's or Parkinson's. There are no guarantees in this world. I can't guarantee that by exercising, you will have zero chance of getting Alzheimer's...but, why not decrease your odds with regular exercise?

I fight with my youngest daughter about this all the time. She hates exercise. She doesn't like physical activity, or sports. We tried a couple things, and she found out that yoga is her jam. We practice five days a week, for seventy-five minutes each day. What's great is that it's a yoga technique that targets stretching and cardio strength, so you kind of get everything wrapped up in one. It's the only class I've ever taken that I liked.

Since taking up yoga, and practicing regularly, I have found I'm more patient. I don't let things rattle my cage as often as they used to before I regularly started practicing yoga. Basically, it keeps me from punching people in the throat! I've seen it ground me, and my girls. My younger daughter, especially, is a bit of a fidgeter. She and I are the same way in that we flit from one thing to another. It's hard for us to stay on task, and I've noticed a big difference in both of us when it comes to our ability to focus and finish what we started.

Physically, my flexibility has improved, as well as my strength and stamina. I can lift heavier weights in the gym at fifty years of age than I could when I was only twenty. I found yoga has been a huge benefit for my greater and improved health. As far as different modalities to gain fitness go, I think yoga is one of the best. But, I also know it's not for everyone. It works for me, because I don't like exercise for exercise's sake.

If you're complaining about your health, and you're a couch potato—think about that. What does a potato look like? A lump. If you want to be a lump, then I guess you sit there and be a couch potato. You can sit there and be on a bunch of medications—that's your choice. But, don't complain to me about your health if you're not taking care of yourself. Yoga may keep me from punching you in the throat, but I will still want to. You'll either become a product of prescription medications which are eventually going to kill you—or, you can actually go out there and get into activity.

In so many ways, I'm kind of like my daughter; I can't stand cross fit. I can't stand spinning. Now, if you love that, then do that. Just make a commitment to yourself for at least three days a week, twenty minutes a day. Even more is better. That regimen has been proven to reduce cholesterol and heart rate while offering better sleep, improving your sex life, and much more. So, don't sit there and tell me you're good if you're not getting up and moving around. You need to make a commitment to yourself. Committing to you is a reflection of your self-worth and self-love. Yes, it's about physical fitness. But, it's also about taking care of yourself, and knowing you are worth the care and attention of exercise.

Working out also increases your metabolic rate which means you have more energy and more stamina for whatever life throws your way. You're able to tackle things, and not feel exhausted by the trials and tribulations we all experience. You'll have more energy to throw into your business and life pursuits. You won't be dragging yourself down, only able to sit on the couch, veg out on Netflix, and not keep up with your household, your family, and your friends.

Fitness is part of our daily life in my family. We work out together. A family that exercises together, stays together. It gives us a great time together to bond. We also sit down for a healthy dinner every single night, no matter what, as a family (when we're not on the road). I think it's imperative that you have family structure and self-structure. What I mean by this is a set schedule of how we spend time together exercising, eating together, and being disciplined in how we take care of ourselves.

I've noticed many individuals in our organization start to take this approach. I see couples working out together in the gym, and families learning better nutrition together. I think this is huge, and it always puts a big grin on my face. I see them transforming their lives, for the better, in all of these pillars we've been discussing. Focusing on fitness as a family, for example, brings balance to the family. Believing in each other's fitness goals as friends strengthens that aspect of life. Plus, everyone feels better!

Your brain is just like your mouth. Your brain consumes information. Your mouth consumes food. So, what you're consuming is going to have a direct correlation on what the output is. If you're eating sewage, reading sewage, and listening to sewage, sewage is going to come out. Garbage in, garbage out. If you eat like crap, you'll feel like crap. If you consume crap for your brain, your brain will spew out crap. No one wants family members and friends who spew crap. You know what else? People won't have faith in you or contribute to your finances either. Drop the crap. Take care of you!

Homework

Where are you, fitness wise? Not just physical, but also emotional—be honest, good and bad:

____

____

____

Where do you want to be fitness wise in one year?

____

____

____

Three years?

____

____

____

Five years?

____

____

____

What are some action steps can you take to balance fitness in your life?

____

____

____

____

____

____

____

____

____

____

Keep looking up… that's the secret of life.

Charlie Brown

Chapter 6

Common Sense and Positivity

People.... please just stop doing dumb shit! Where has common sense gone in our society? It left the building! I mean, look at some of the lawsuits that are filed, or some of the crap that's posted on social media. Let's talk about some of the crap that's on CNN and Fox news. It's really ridiculous. Look at the news channels—who do they interview when they look to interview somebody? It's usually the dumbest person in the crowd.

I stopped watching television news a long time ago. The only time I have to be subjected to that crap is when I am out in public, at the gym in the sauna, or at a restaurant. In addition to much of the news being fake, it's constantly negative. What bleeds, leads. So, I don't invite that stupidity and negativity into my home. It's the same with social media. When I see something really stupid or negative, I block it. Think about it, this type of media can be used for immense social good, and instead, it's often used for irrelevant subjects and materials.

One of my biggest peeves is when people get on social media and air all their dirty laundry, or whatever is bothering them today, this week, and this month. Here's the truth of the matter: no one cares. If you want to get sympathy votes, have at it. But, I think it's a waste of everyone's time. We all have bad times and tough times. Why broadcast them on social media? Personally, I think people do it to get attention—even if it's negative attention.

I get it. Maybe you want someone to commiserate with. Again, misery loves company. But, what's the point? How does being negative on social media bring ANY positivity to your life? It may get people to feel sorry for you. Is that what you really want? Maybe it will get you some attention. Is that the kind of attention you really want? If you're suffering from the "Oh, woe is me" syndrome, common sense has left the building, and that's 80% of our society.

It goes right into the correlation of positive living that I see over, and over, and over again in my line of work. 20 percent of the people are making money, 80 percent are not.

And, that 20 percent making the money, are making 80 percent of the money.

Mind your mind. What are you putting out there in your world? Are you putting out thoughts, feelings and actions that are going to bring positivity to your world? Or, are you "woe is meing?" If you're doing that, then you're draining your own energy, and the energy of those around you. I guarantee it, even if they don't say anything to you about it. Hell, maybe they're so down, they don't even notice it.

I'm not trying to beat you up if this is pushing a button. I just want to be honest with what I see, and how I can help people break this terrible negative pattern. I honestly think that negativity and common sense are tied together at the hip. If you are in one realm, then you are dragging along the other. If you hear something negative about something, use common sense and don't just listen to what you're hearing. Take the time to shake things off, dive in deep and do your research. And, don't just look for things you agree with, use your common sense to look for information that is real and honest, then make your own determination.

There are a million talking heads in the world, especially nowadays. Anyone can start a blog, or a YouTube Channel, or a "news" channel, and guess what?...everyone does! Many times, the people who start them are people with little or no experience, or common sense themselves. And, they know that 80 percent of the country will tune in and swallow their line of bullshit—hook, line and sinker. And, most of the time, the talking heads are just bantering about, playing the blame game, shouting, “He did this.” “She did that.” “It’s their fault.”

You know what? The blame game’s over. Don’t play it anymore. I don’t play it anymore. I am responsible for my own behavior. I am responsible for the words that come out of my mouth. I am responsible for my actions. No one else is responsible. Not my husband, not my kids, not my business, not my team, not my business partners. I am responsible. Say that out loud. “I am responsible.” Own it.

The basis for common sense is this. You are responsible. If you screw up, you’re responsible. If you succeed, you’re responsible. It’s not so-and-so’s fault, nor is it so-and-so’s responsibility. The only thing you can really, truly control in your life is you, and no one or nothing else. The thing I notice, over and over again, is to look at what people do when they’re struggling—financially and otherwise. Most of the time, they’re complaining and gossiping.

Turn that around. If people who are struggling are constantly negative, be constantly positive. Most of the time things work out how they’re supposed to, or at least in a way where you can learn something and maybe keep your heart and mind open to something even better that comes your way.

Take a look at the people who AREN'T successful in life. Consider their life patterns. What do they do? What mistakes do they make? What are they saying? How are they acting? If you want to bring positivity and more success into your life, look at what they're doing, and do the opposite. You can absolutely reverse engineer success.

People who are struggling, (the 80 percent) are typically doing all the wrong stuff. They're looking at successful people in a negative light. They're reading the wrong crap. They're watching the wrong crap. They're eating the wrong crap. They're always comparing themselves to successful people, but they never put two and two together, and recognize their own unhealthy, negative patterns. Comparing yourself to someone else is one of the biggest dream stealers.

People awake from their own slumber of negativity, usually when things have gotten so bad, they have no other choice but to do things differently. If they're lucky, or rather smart, they realize they have to do things in a completely different way. They have to realize they are the only ones in control. Therefore, they are the only ones who can do things differently for themselves. They either have to pick themselves up, and put on a new hat in life, or just move away from whatever it is that is holding them down. Whether it's a dead-end job, or a deadbeat spouse.

Sometimes I'm the messenger who shows up at the right time in their life. I don't spout anything new or groundbreaking, but they've heard the message time and time and time again, and finally this time, it hits them. It makes sense. The pieces come together, and the future looks different. But, it's the one person that says something, or shows something, and the other person is at the right point in their life where they're open to finally hearing it for the first time. When people are in a negative space, they're usually closed off. There's nothing you can say or do to help them see a way out.

When you become "comfortable" with a paycheck to paycheck life, or an "ok" relationship, you are staying in negativity. You have shut down your common sense, because common sense would tell you to get the fuck out. You aren't seeing new opportunities, and you start comparing yourself to others. Maybe you see that retired educator, with her vacation home in Belize and her boat in Florida "living the life." You get jealous. You think what she has is unattainable. But, that's bull. Common sense means you take a look at her life, and you figure out how to make it your own. Not by complaining, or comparing, but reverse engineering what she did so that you can find your own "living the lifestyle."

We're taught to settle, aren't we? That retired educator was taught that too. She got married at a young age (I think around twenty years old), because she dated her future husband for four years. "What's next?" she said. "I guess we should get married." "I guess we should buy that little ranch in the boondocks." "I guess I should work this job and get a business degree, because that's what they'll pay for." "I guess I should stay married, even though I'm incredibly unhappy."

It took her moving to another state, with her husband, and pursuing her dream job of an educator. After a couple years, she was divorced, and independent for the first time in her adult life. She loved her teaching job, and then moved into administrator positions. She bought her own little ranch house, right in the middle of everything. She purchased a ranch property, to fulfill her dream of having tons of space and room—all with no mortgage and no debt. She didn't settle for waiting until she could retire at age 65. Instead, by the age of fifty, she was retired, and working for herself. Within five years, with her new life partner, she enjoys "the good life" BECAUSE she didn't settle.

Why should we ever settle for mediocrity? Just do "this" and you can work for forty years and get your Timex. Hell, that doesn't even happen anymore. The days of a corporation being loyal to lifelong employees are over. How about, instead, work for four months, and buy your own Rolex?

Back when things were really financially pathetic for my husband and I (he lost fifty percent of his income, and I was between business opportunities and didn't have any money coming in either) we went through all of our savings. We were living in Chicago at the time, and sold everything we could to survive. At one point, he had to sell his Rolex so we could make ends meet. It was a terrible blow for him, and maybe one of our lowest points financially. Here we had succeeded to a certain level, and pretty much thought all was going to be ok.

We refused to give into the negativity, and worked our butts off to get back on track financially and otherwise. We worked together to get our finances back in shape, and finally found the perfect business arrangement and partner to do that. After just a few years, we were in a better position—far surpassing anything we had before. Again, a case of things happening for the better, even if we had to go through some pretty shitty times. As one of my friends says, "If one door closes, another opens—it's just the hallway that sucks sometimes."

He was able to retire early, since our business venture took off. That Father's Day, I took him to the Rolex dealer in town. We paid cash for a brand-new Submariner Rolex watch for him. At first, he didn't want it. I said to him, "I want to buy this for you...I need you to do this *for me*." It was just one of those things. Yes, it was a materialistic thing, but it really meant something to me. He had his original Rolex watch before we got together. He had it when we first had financial hardships, and I knew it was so hard for him to let that go. But he did what he needed to do to support our family. The first thing I wanted to do for him, to show ourselves how we could and did remain positive throughout those financial problems, was to get him that watch back—or, at least one just like it.

He sold that watch to help us put food on the table. At the time he sold it, I was in a really bad space, and in some ways, him selling that watch saved my life. In my darkest days, he sacrificed that watch. The watch wasn't just an item. It was a symbol, now lost, of success and a happier time. I can't even imagine how hard that must have been for him. He also had to sell his boat, which was another heartbreaker. Again, it wasn't so much about the material ownership of objects or things. It was about pride, and the distress of putting that pride aside to save the family.

If we had fallen into negativity, and let our financial problems get us down, and not tapped into our common sense, I'm pretty sure I wouldn't be sitting here writing this book. We would probably be really struggling, thinking we had to go back to 9-5 jobs, trapped in a gray city, with crappy weather. We would be unhappy. We might not even still be together, since most divorces come out of financial stress and hardship. Thank goodness we kept our heads above water, and didn't allow ourselves to drown in our own tears. For his

50th birthday, we bought his dream boat. And yes, we paid cash for it!

I had to shut out the naysayers in my life to get to where we are today. I had a million people tell me, "No, that business idea is ridiculous," or "You're just going to go deeper in debt than you already are," or "That will never work." I had people tell me to not marry my husband. Or, move to a warmer climate. Or pursue our dream of becoming independently wealthy. These people were all around me, and they are part of the negativity I eliminated in my life.

At some point, you just have to shut those voices off. You just have to trust your own common sense and dream bigger, and what you know is good for you and your partner and family. You have to listen to what your brain and heart tells you will work. Sometimes you'll trip up and "fail," but you still have to have faith in yourself and who and what you want to be. There are no shortcuts to this. You have to fail sometimes. My current network marketing opportunity, which has been so immensely successful, came only after I failed three times before. THREE times! But, I had faith in knowing I could succeed at this, and I trust my common sense and my gut.

Before I joined our current organization, I was told, "No, don't. You need to get a real job." Sure, I would have been "ok" with a real job. I could have settled. I could still be living in

Chicago. I could be renting an apartment or a house, because we couldn't afford to buy one. But, hey, we're "ok." That wasn't an option because my gut, my intuition, and my core was telling me to partner with this company. I also knew I would freaking kick my own ass if I didn't jump on the opportunity. And, I would have. Because that opportunity led me to here. I'm in a place where I'm helping people, publishing books, and coaching individuals to strive past what they ever thought possible in life. It's allowed me to open up my speaking platform, and now leading to even more.

I can help people have that "lightbulb" moment. I can hold people accountable. I am a professional accountability partner, because I don't let people beat around the bush. I don't let people sugarcoat things, and I go straight between the eyes. I really feel like you need to know yourself, and if you can answer the questions of who you are, where you have been, and where you're going, common sense will follow. That's where it comes from. It comes from that notion of self-love, and self-love comes from knowing who you are, warts and all, and knowing what you need to do to achieve your dreams.

Common sense, through knowing yourself, is actually very simple. It's not rocket science. When we strip away all the layers—and keep things effing simple—we can find this very easily. Too often we create too many layers of confusion, and you know what? I'm sick of it. It's just time to get down to common sense.

For example, in schools and at home, in my opinion, they're teaching all the wrong stuff. Finally, though, I think we're seeing more and more practical education. For example, I think it's important to bring back the value of the trades. But, still, we don't teach our kids how to think for themselves and how to solve their own problems. Independent thought is critical for success! We don't teach our kids holistically. I understand we have to teach history, and math, and reading/writing skills, for example. But, to sit and drone on and on about two hundred years of history, for example, gets us nowhere if we don't teach the skills to help our kids contribute to society, learn from our history, and help us move forward in a positive way.

Instead, let's talk about how to solve current issues. Let's teach our kids how to be leaders, how to empower themselves, and how to balance a damn checkbook. Let's teach our kids how to tap into the positive. Let's teach our kids how to be critical thinkers, so they can sift through the crap that social media, and what society in general throws at us. How can we help them learn how to contribute to their lives now, and the quality of their lives now and into the future? If we're not teaching them about real life, how are they going to do in life? We have to be their advocates, but we also have to teach them how to take the ropes for themselves.

Instead of rolling our eyes about how there's no common sense, what are we doing, as the adults in the room, to help our kids develop that common sense? Are we making excuses for them, and enabling their behavior, or are we helping them learn from their mistakes and feel the consequences of those mistakes? Are we giving them a hand-out, or a hand-up? Are we encouraging them to explore their world? Are we pushing college and university education, when maybe their interests are elsewhere? Let's help our kids develop common sense by not holding their hands so tight they're afraid to explore life on their own, and on their own terms and live out their dreams instead of parents trying to live vicariously through their eyes!! We need to listen and talk *with* our children not *at* them.

Homework

How do you maintain positivity in your life?

Where are you lacking in positivity? In which area(s) of your life, for example, do you need to be more positive?

How can you encourage the development of common sense in yourself, and those around you?

Education without application is just entertainment.

Tim Sanders

Chapter 7

Mindful Learning and Finding a Purpose

Here's the thing...learning has to be where your true interests are. Mindful learning is a lifelong commitment and habit. It means you're not learning stuff that's counter-productive to what you know you should be doing. So, let's say you went to school to be an engineer. In order to be an engineer in certain fields, you need a master's degree. Let's say you have a bachelor's degree, and you're a civil engineer. And, you hate it. Why the hell would you go to school for another two or three years for something you hate? You're wasting your time. You're wasting your money. You're not following your life's passion and spark. In other words, you're settling.

Mindful learning is learning something that is your life's purpose. I'm thinking of my friend I mentioned earlier, who was pursuing a degree in business management. She hated it. Every chance she could, she took electives related to education and the study of environmental biology. Those were her real passions. When she was faced with her third accounting course, she woke up and told me, "I hated these courses—not because I wasn't good at them—I was. It just didn't interest me one tiny, little bit. I wanted to be an educator."

Everybody has a purpose. Some people have multiple purposes. Maybe their purpose is fulfilled through their business, their family, or a favorite charity. There are multiple motivators and drivers that can point you to your true purpose. Everything you do to make yourself a better person, including education, should lead you to that purpose. If you're feeling frustrated that you don't have a purpose, mindful learning can lead you to that purpose. For example, how many people do you know who started college with a degree or major in mind, only to switch it up after they took an elective, or even a required course that piqued their interest and passions much more than their original stated major?

My friend, the educator, tells me, "When I first started college, I took all the mandatory core courses; psychology, history, life sciences, literature. I loved them all. I 'switched' my major every semester." She laughs, "I mean, not really, but I fell in love with all of them. I considered majoring in psychology, biology, history—anything but business, and maybe math!"

Mindful learning begins with at least ten minutes of personal and professional development, every day. At least! You need to be listening to podcasts to speak to your life purpose. You need to be reading and reflecting on material, smart material, each and every day. Substituting mindful learning for a minimum of ten minutes every day can be balanced with activities like studying music, or dancing (which is one of the best mood elevators, ever). Learning is like food, it's either fuel or garbage. Your mind operates the same way.

We all have the same twenty-four hours in a day. The average teen to young adult spends almost seven hours in front of a screen—whether it's a television screen, a computer screen or their phone. Grown adults are even worse—spending as many as 10 hours every day behind a screen.[3] How many times have you seen a couple, or a family, out to dinner with everyone looking at their screens instead of talking and communicating with each other? The dinner table is NO place for screens EVER! Replacing even just half of screen time with mindful learning, will help you get to your place of purpose and life success in a much shorter time.

Mindful learning is also getting into action for things you want to accomplish. When you've reached a goal you've set, and you've figured out how to do it, you have that experience and you have the learning part of that down. But, that's not when and how mindful learning stops. Mindful learning should be continuous. Now, what do you have to learn? Now where do you need to go? Maybe now you can take that mindful learning and go teach/share with someone else what you've learned, and what you now know. Teaching enhances, even more, your level of learning. It's said that the best way to learn something fully and completely is by teaching it to someone else. That's when full mastery develops.

If you are clear about your life's purpose; where you want to go, who you want to do that with, then whenever life presents you with something that might be a challenge, or a blip, you can see it as an opportunity. Since you're living mindful learning, you probably have a solution in mind, or you know the right people and right ideas that get you through, up, and over that speed bump. Mindful learning is being aware of where you're going so when something presents itself, you know how to use your knowledge and experience.

Filling your mind with mindful books, podcasts, and anything else that contributes to mindful learning, keeps you on your toes. You're always ready to deal with whatever comes your way. More importantly, this knowledge can help you identify problems before they become a problem. You're able to almost predict the future, because you're mindful of your life, and what's going on because you are in control. You can avoid problems because you see them far before you would have without mindful learning experiences.

Mindful learning isn't just about sitting around and listening. It's also about action—going out and putting your knowledge into action. It can be about going to different workshops and programs, buying coaching or mentoring packages, attending seminars, and participating in discussions. Mindful learning is about investing in yourself and your learning. However, you have to be careful about a lot of those coaching programs. Most of them are shit, and most people find out the hard way. Do your research, and be smart about where you put your money.

Where you put your money is where you put your energy. Where you put your energy is where things can happen. That's not to say that you must spend a lot of money to get to a place of mindful learning. There's a lot of really good quality free content out there. I call it YouTube University! Of course, there's a lot of crap in the free world, too. But it's a place to start. It's a place where you can go to get ideas, and sift through what feels like a fit for you. When you're ready, go to live events so that you can surround yourself with like-minded people.

When you surround yourself with like-minded individuals, they have similar goals, and they want to be more successful. These opportunities are, very often, a dose of positivity. Feeding your mind is like feeding your body—good, clean energy. Whenever you can feed your mind with a clean nutritious diet of information, the more clear your ideals, purpose, and motivations become.

Mindful learning is also learning what NOT to do. When you make a mistake, or maybe jump into an opportunity that is NOT a good fit, mindful learning teaches you to actually learn from that—and, not to blame it on others or even yourself. It's just learning. And it becomes mindful when you have a certain level of consciousness during these types of experiences.

When I think back on the two network marketing positions that almost destroyed me financially, I realize that if I had not been in a mindset of deliberate, mindful learning, I would have just chalked things up as a failure, and never grown from there. With a start-up, for example, you have to be fast and furious. That includes some kind of template that you can shoot off from. Thanks to that "failure," part of my mindful learning was making sure I had a template in place before I jumped into my next network marketing opportunity. Since then, I've created hundreds of templates for others to use in their mindful learning.

The Universe loves momentum, so when you're ready to go, the door opens. Preparing yourself to be in that state of readiness requires mindful learning through formal, informal, and experiential opportunities. Once you have momentum, it is self-perpetuating. But, you have to pay attention! You have to keep learning. Because, once that momentum slows down or stops, it's really hard, infinitely more difficult to get things going once again. Mindful learning, habitually, keeps that momentum and drive going to almost infinite possibilities.

What's in motion stays in motion. The Universe IS motion. Once you get momentum, you need momentum and motivation to stay in motion. One keyway to do that is to find that balance in your life, as we've already discussed with family, friends, finances, fitness, and faith. Part of achieving that balance, a HUGE part of getting there, is through the power of mindful learning.

When my friend Marianne passed away, things really changed for me. Marianne was an amazing woman who touched many lives. She passed away fairly quickly. When she died, it kind of caught everyone off guard. Some folks, when they heard of her passing, hadn't even known she was very sick.

Over five hundred people attended her memorial service. She knew so many people—and this was before social media. All of us packed into a little, tiny church to say our goodbyes. It was then when I realized that my purpose was to be like Marianne. I committed to being someone who truly cared about people, do something I love, and provide others a valuable service. At the time, I didn't necessarily know what that "something" was, and couldn't have imagined that it would lead me to where I am now, but that moment has always stayed with me.

Marianne passed away many years ago, way before I found out network marketing was my jam. With Marianne as my model, the more self-actualized I became, the more I realized my life path was to use network marketing as my vehicle to reach out to as many people as I could. And, through network marketing, it can happen exponentially because it's not just me doing it—it's my team and my network marketing family. My team has nearly a quarter of a million members! That's one hell of an impact.

Finding my purpose comes in waves. So much of how I define my purpose is about timing. For example, earlier I spoke of the community centers in Colombia. If that opportunity to contribute had presented itself two or three years ago, I don't think I would have been there. Honestly, I don't think I would have connected with it, and realized, "Ah, here is another reason I'm here." It's all about timing, and being ready to recognize and accept that there is a greater purpose for your existence on this planet. Timing is everything.

Whether you want to admit it or not, time is the one commodity we can't get back. You can always get back your health. You can always get back money. Those things you can lose, and gain them, and lose them, and gain them again. But, you can never lose and gain time.

Over the years, I've learned to value time, and it's the number one gift I can give people. And, their time is the greatest gift they can give me. Sometimes people just need someone to listen to them, and as long as they're not whining, and we're coming up with solutions, I will give them all the time they need. I like to listen and help people realize they are valued. So often, we forget about the listening part of communication.

Sometimes people just need a pat on the shoulder, or a hug, or maybe just a simple smile. Simply remembering someone's name, and saying their name when I see them again makes a difference. That simple act can literally change their life—you just never know. This is why I'm always stopping to talk with people and engage with them. That's one of my purposes in life.

Life is about building relationships. This matters for our personal lives, as well as our business lives. If we forget that all important aspect of having a meaningful purpose in life, we can't build anything. We certainly can't build a self-sustaining, successful business without seeing relationships, listening, and caring as important reasons to be in business. Of course, we can't build meaningful personal relationships without emphasizing this notion, either. If you're to build purpose in life, but you're ignoring the importance of creating, maintaining, and nurturing quality relationships, then I think you're really missing the boat.

I see too many entrepreneurs try to fake this. They pretend to care. They pretend the other person is important to them. They pretend they value relationships, honesty, integrity, and meaningful communication. But, you know what? Smart people can see and feel fakery from a mile away. Don't be that dick. DBTD

Homework

What does mindful learning mean to you?

____

____

____

How can you improve yourself through mindful learning? Set some specific goals:

____

____

____

What are some specific actions that can help you fulfill the above goals?

____

____

____

Income seldom exceeds personal development.

Jim Rohn

Chapter 8

Personal and Professional Growth

What drives you to succeed? What holds you back? When you have such a strong desire to move forward with something that it causes you to not be able to sleep at night, that's something to really look at. What are you passionate about? How does personal and professional growth help you go after that passion and that drive? 90 percent of people who have achieved great success in life have gone through some sort of significant struggle in life. Nothing substantial is achieved without a struggle, and learning from those struggles via personal and professional development is, I think, the key to really exceeding all your expectations about how far you can go in life. Development and desire creates hunger.

I believe you have to work twice as hard on yourself as you do in your business. If you want your life to grow, your business to grow, and your wealth to grow, YOU have to grow. YOU have to accept that mediocrity is crap, and you have to step out of accepting mediocrity in your life, ever again. Personal and professional growth is a non-negotiable when it comes to life and business success. When you're growing, your business is growing. When you are learning and taking on something new, you're creating new neural pathways in your brain. This means you're becoming smarter and more flexible in your thinking.

Before I started working on my own personal development, people, I was a bitch. You would not have liked me at all. Believe it or not, I was negative. I blamed everything and everyone else for my "problems." I ate like crap. I watched crap TV. I read crap books. Garbage in, garbage out, like I said earlier. My life was miserable. I was miserable. And, the people around me were miserable.

For me, a huge part of my personal growth was really understanding, and feeling gratitude. As I learned to strip the garbage out of my life, and see the wonderful things that could, would, and will happen in my life, things changed. I could open my eyes in the morning with that sense of wonderment. Before that, I was waking up dead. Not literally, of course, but dead to that beauty, dead to that potential, and dead to that feeling of gratitude. What empty days I had back then.

How does gratitude look in your life? It could be telling someone you are thinking of them. It could be paying it forward by buying a cup of coffee for someone you don't know (yet). It can be letting cars pass you on the highway. It could be a simple smile, or a "Hello" offered to a stranger. Gratitude is about building a positive relationship with yourself, and passing that along to others. It can be a kind word, or just focusing on someone else's strengths and gifts. Even the people you don't like have something positive to offer the world. See that, instead of how you "think" they don't stack up. Judgment is the opposite of gratitude.

Growth and gratitude come from personal development. For example, I read every day. I listen to positive and meaningful podcasts—every day. I reach out to new people, every day. I think this is important for personal and professional development. If we are constantly working on building and maintaining positive relationships in our life, then this personal and professional growth will happen naturally.

I think, especially in network marketing, but really in any business that deals with other human beings—which is all of them, ultimately it becomes critical to focus on gratitude. People want to do business with people that they know, like, and trust. You can't take a shortcut to developing quality personal relationships. You have to invest time and energy to develop this in your personal and professional life. And then, I guarantee you, you will see your business grow.

For example, I encourage members of our team to meet new people—every day. Whether that's on social media, or just connecting in their everyday activities, it doesn't matter. Let's think of the coffee shop, for example. If you go and get a cup of coffee at a local cafe every day, you will start to see the same people there. Strike up a simple conversation. Compliment them on their outfit, or just say "Hi!" Make eye contact, smile, and brighten someone else's day. Not only will this help you stretch out of your comfort zone, it's a way to grow personally and professionally.

As you get to know someone, and you feel a connection or a positive vibe coming from them, invite them to connect further. Get connected via social media, and follow-up with them by a voice text, or a phone call. Side note: if you are "connecting" with people via typed private or direct messages on social media, you've just lost all your credibility. Nothing connects better than a follow-up with the enthusiasm in your voice.

If you are in ANY type of business, I don't care which type, you have to always be looking for new customers. You have to grow, or you will die as a business. The way to do this is to develop meaningful relationships. Be the person that people like, know, and trust. Start those conversations, develop those relationships, and keep them. It's much easier to retain a client than to get new ones, even though you have to be doing both. But, don't be on the hunt. If someone senses you're seeing them ONLY as a prospect, they will run like their Mach 5 hair is on fire.

No. Develop these relationships, and make them real. Insincerity can be spotted from a mile away. If you are open and honest at the get-go, about what you do, and who you are, people will be more drawn to you. For instance, I always let people know, right away who I am. I introduce myself by saying, "I'm the queen of network marketing. I love what I do—and I get paid to wash my hair, y'all!" I've never, and I mean never, been told by someone to "Eff off and never contact me again," when I reach out about our business opportunity. I think that's because I don't stalk and I don't preach. I just am who I am. I'm sincere, honest, and trustworthy.

When you're in business, and looking to build and grow your clientele, you will get twenty "No" responses for every "Yes." That's the breaks—that's life. Don't take it personally—they're not saying No" to you. They're just saying "No, not right now" to your product, service or opportunity. In general, a person says "No" seven times before they'll ever consider saying "Yes." And, guess what? Most business owners give up after the first three "No" responses. That's short-sighted, to say the least. (If you need help dealing with objections, check out my resource, "Objections are Invitations" here: **bit.ly/TVInvitations**.)

I encourage you to reach out to at least three people, daily. Not to "prospect," not to "sell." Just to connect. Start building those relationships. Spend time with each other. Don't push through and try to get to the chase with anything. Let the relationship develop naturally and organically. Grow your business by investing in your personal development. Relationship building is why we're all put on this planet. Make someone's day by letting them know you're thinking about them. Maybe that will develop into a professional connection, and if it does, great. But, you must let those connections lead where they lead. If you're loving what you do, and you're successful, people will naturally want to get in on it, knowing you'll be there to mentor and grow with them.

I think we all have leaders inside of us. Being a leader isn't about having a title. It's about what you do, and how you treat others. In everything you say and do, is it true? Is it helpful? Is it done with integrity? Is it kind? When you're practicing these tenets, you are a leader, and people will be drawn to you. I can lay my head on my pillow knowing I act and speak with integrity. Maybe it's sometimes what people don't want to do or hear, but that's not my problem. As long as

I'm in integrity, and I'm being kind and respectful to those around me, I know that I am growing as an individual, and as I grow, my business does the same.

Homework

What are you grateful for in your life?

Who are some leaders you admire?

How do you plan on growing your business? Detail some of your initial ideas:

Individual commitment to a group effort--that is what makes a teamwork, a company work, a society work, a civilization work.

Vince Lombardi

Chapter 9

Teamwork

Teamwork isn't just about your business, or network marketing. In my family—we're a team. It takes teamwork to make the dream work. You can't get anywhere on your own.

If it's just you and your dog, you're a team. Maybe you're single, and your parents have passed away, and it's just you and a sibling—you're a team. It takes a team to do things on a grand scale. It takes just one person to have an idea, but it takes a great team to do great things with that idea. A team can be you and one other person. It is *The Power of One* (great book by the way).

Teamwork is about being consistent—and that means being consistent no matter what. As John D. Rockefeller said, "I would rather earn 1% of 100 people's efforts than 100% of my own efforts." He's so right. In terms of teamwork, I would rather have 100 members of my team, each doing 1% of what is needed, than me doing 100% of the work.

Think about a broken-down car or truck. It might take two, three, or four people to push that car out of the road. Then, what happens as that car builds momentum and speed? It keeps rolling. Those people don't need to push nearly as hard as it took to get the car rolling. That's teamwork. Each person has to push as hard as they can at the beginning of the process, but then as things get rolling, they can let up their efforts exponentially.

In any team, in any effort, things start to inevitably slow down. Also, it's more likely than not that you'll have 20% of the team producing 80% of the results. That's ok. That's natural. It helps build sustainability into your team, and sometimes those players trade-off roles, as your team grows and evolves. Massive growth, and sustaining that growth is impossible without a team.

Earlier in my career, I refused to work in or create a team. I was egotistical, and had to do everything myself. You might say I was a bit of a control freak. But, it takes a lot of time to do all that, and it takes time away from income generating activities. Finally, I started hiring assistants, including virtual assistants. I was able to delegate tasks to my team, and focus myself on activities that generated my paycheck. And…my paycheck when up when I hired people to do the things I don't like or don't do well.

If you're working at home, and getting things up and running in your business, as soon as you start getting busy, and find tasks taking up income producing activities, and hire helpers. The first thing I recommend is hiring a housekeeper to come at least every other week. They can help you keep up on your home and household, while you work on earning income.

Then, as you get busier, hire more assistants. Hire someone to do research for you, or put your ideas into documents that you can use for speaking engagements, or selling your opportunity. Remember, you're not letting go of control, you're controlling your activities with the help of a team.

Make sure that your team is helping you free up time so you can grow and invest in your business. Team members can help you find more time. Remember time is a commodity you can never get back. The most successful people I know invest in services that save them time—time they can use to continue to grow their personal and professional lives. Simply put, outsource your weaknesses. Outsource things that don't directly put wealth into your pocket. Surround yourself with people better than you.

A good team can help keep your spirits up, and help you grow personally and professionally by balancing out a crappy day. You become a product of your team. My worth is based off of our entire team. A rising tide lifts all boats. Our team is our tide. Our network marketing team has created 25 multi-millionaires. There are 600 people in our organization making more than six figures. Thanks to network marketing, 50,000 families on our team are earning an extra $200 or $300 a month. That amount can help someone keep from foreclosing on their home or bankrupting themselves. That's the rising tide of our team, and a telling example of what we accomplished in just five years.

When you're building a team, don't reinvent the wheel. There's no reason for you to start from scratch. There are people in your industry who are successful and active. Find them. Emulate them. Learn from them. Don't ever pay for a "guru." Most of the time they're not active in the business. They're woefully out of touch and full of shit. You will learn much, much more by modeling your actions and behaviors after people who have been there and succeed before you. These people are a part of your team, too.

Bottom line, I wouldn't be where I am without a team. I don't know of anyone who really succeeded in life without building a team, and being a thoughtful, respectful, driving leader. I win by leading through example and leading with an open heart and an open mind. I never forget to show respect and value for all team members. The notion of team as simply a group of people who help you get things done is outdated. A team lifts you, and you lift them. This is the beauty of recognizing and creating a wonderful team—in your life, in your community, and in your business. And there is also an art of letting people lead. No matter what there are always opportunities for leadership. At home, in school, in a career, the possibilities are endless.

Homework

Define what teamwork means to you:

____

____

____

Describe a time when you were on a great team. What made it great?

____

____

____

Describe a time when you were on a crappy team. What made it crappy?

____

____

In your team, however it's defined, how are you contributing in a positive way? How can you improve?

____

____

____

When you arise in the morning,

think of what a precious privilege it is to be alive

- to breathe, to think, to enjoy, to love.

Marcus Aurelius

Chapter 10

Daily Action Steps/Tasks

I was talking to one of my business associates about the different levels she could achieve in the organization, and how she was well on her way. "I know I'll get there, eventually," she exclaimed.

"That's not good enough," I told her. "You need to put a date on it. Tell me, WHEN will you get there?"

She smiled, knowing what I was doing. I preach over and over about putting timelines on our goals.

"December 31," she added.

"December 31 of what…" I pushed further.

"December 31 of this year." she finished.

"Alright, it's go-time, girl!" I said. At the time, it was just as I was writing this book, in the fall of that same year. "Ok, you've got two and a half months to be at this level. You've made a commitment to yourself. You work your action plan backwards, and this is exactly what you need to do. We've got to find you two more people who will run with you. You need [xx] amount of volume. You can absolutely do this. We're coming into the fourth quarter, our busiest time of the year..."

You can put together the best action plan, set up daily tasks, and learn how to work your action plan backwards to achieve the goals you set. DMO'S (daily method of operation) are the backbone of getting things done. But, if you don't have a date, a deadline, and a SPECIFIC timeline for your goal, how do you expect to plan for it?

We're notorious, as a society, for not doing this. Listen, I love vision boards, for example. You have to put out your goals and visions. But, you also have to plan to achieve them, and put timelines and deadlines on yourself. Otherwise, you've just created a pretty board that means nothing.

I knew one woman who spent more than $100,000 on an advanced degree at a prestigious graduate school. She could have gotten a job ANYWHERE, doing what she dreamed of doing, which was international marketing. After she graduated, her dream was to work in South America, a continent at the time that was ripe for exactly her expertise and talents.

But, that's as far as she got. It was a dream. She literally said to me one time, "I know someone will just contact me, and make that connection for me." She put absolutely no effort into networking with people who COULD make that connection for her. Nor did she put herself out there, in any manner, shape or form, to be noticed by someone who could connect her. It was a dream. It was a vision. And, it got her nowhere. Almost twenty years later, she's stuck in basically the same corporate, dead-end job she had before she got her very expensive diploma.

If you've ever met me, or know anything about how I work with people, you know I have absolutely no patience for people who say, "Well, I'll just try…" or "I'll just see how it goes." That's the biggest line of bullshit you can ever say to me. And, you know what? It's not a line of BS you're telling me. You're bullshitting yourself, more than anyone else. You're bullshitting your family and your friends. You're not really trying, and you clearly don't have a plan. That's not how life works, now is it?

Every day, I think it's critical to have a routine of what you will do to get yourself ready to tackle life, as it hits. I have seven simple things I do each day to get my mind, spirit, and body ready for the day, and for whatever I have planned, as well as whatever shows up that's not planned. Developing healthy habits that help you balance out your life is probably one of the best things you can do for yourself.

In order to have rich relationships and rewarding business activities, it's important to ensure daily actions are intentional and geared toward success, rather than mindless and haphazard.

For the past three years, I've been incorporating the following seven daily success starters to achieve personal balance and increase income. It's working!

Hal Elrod's book, The Miracle Morning, was so eye-opening for me. It helped me establish a morning routine that gets my day off to a good start while creating momentum for success.

Begin your day with the following Success Starters:

1. **Give Thanks**—Immediately upon waking up (even before getting out of bed), give thanks for another day, remind yourself how awesome you are, and note everything you're grateful for.

2. **Feed Your Brain**—Read at least 10 pages of a personal or professional development book to engage your brain and learn what's new. Leaders are readers and must stay on top of new material.

3. **Move Your Body**—My exercise of choice is yoga. It helps me (and my girls) gain clarity, have focus, and stay flexible. As an added bonus, it keeps me from punching others when I'm frustrated.

With appreciation in my heart, a focused brain, and a revved up body, I'm ready to start my work day. There are two tasks I complete every day that are integral to my business success. They are:

4. **Connect**—Make a point to introduce yourself to two new people every single day. The best connections are natural and take place when you're living your life. I meet people at the yoga studio, when I'm traveling, at the grocery store, and online through social media. Be who you are, while representing your business in every interaction. This doesn't mean sell every person you meet, but make a genuine connection. As I mentioned, people buy from people they know and trust.

5. **Reach Out**—Follow up on business items. This could be servicing customers, following up with prospects, answering emails, and calling people in your downline. The Rule of Seven notes people need to be exposed to a product or service at least seven times before they make a purchase. Having genuine connections and following up in an authentic way helps facilitate the buying process.

Two of the seven success starters make the first five possible and are ever present every day. They are:

6. **Eat Well**—It's important to fill your body with good, healthy food. The foods you eat fuel your body and give you energy to make it through the day. Just as we put performance fuels in our car, it's important to fill the vehicle of the body with foods that sustain and maintain it for success.

7. **Rest Well**—The National Sleep Foundation recommends adults get seven to nine hours of sleep every day. Getting adequate rest keeps the crankiness away, while providing energy to generate success.

Try these 7 Daily Success Starters for 90 days and let me know how different your life and business look. I promise you'll see a noticeable change.

It's a bit of an exaggeration when people say it takes 21 days to develop a new habit. I think that's hogwash. It takes at least 60 to 90 days. And I mean consistency, for 60 to 90 days, in order to change something in your life. In order to do this, you have to give yourself the grace of space, and the grace of time. Just because you start something, like a New Year's Resolution, if you give up after two weeks, you'll see no results. But, if you're consistent for 30, 60, 90 days, you'll really start seeing results. Stay consistent for another 30, 60, or 90 days, and now you're talking about six months of effort that will really pay off.

You may not even recognize the old you, at that point. Other people will start to see it, and they'll start telling you how amazing you look, or how much energy you seem to have. They'll notice, and comment on your positive outlook on life, and exclaim "How do you do it?!"

Homework

What is your daily routine for success? Is it working for you? If so, why? If not, why not?

____

____

____

What kind of new healthy and positive habit do you want to develop?

____

____

____

Describe some action steps for building that habit over the next month?

____

____

____

____

____

____

____

Love yourself unconditionally, just as you love those closest to you despite their faults.

Les Brown

Final Thoughts

Self-Love and Self-Worth

I've touched on this throughout the book; the importance of self-love, self-esteem, self-confidence and self-worth. How do you become more self-actualized?

At the end of the day, especially for women, we're taught to give and give and give, in spite of our own needs, and in spite of ourselves. Yes, we need to live with a higher purpose in mind. No question we should think of others, but not at the cost of ourselves. These two aspects are not mutually exclusive. You can think of yourself, and others at the same time.

This reminds me of a concept of mutual respect. Most of the time, we think of mutual respect in a highly conditional way. What I mean by this is that our general definition of mutual respect, if I were to ask most people, would be something along the lines of, "I will respect you if you respect me," or "I respect you, so you should respect me."

I think a greater way to look at this, in this notion of "self" is a tad different. Instead of the respect being conditional—"if" you respect me—it should be a little more "self" focused. Basically, "I respect myself, AND I respect you." Think about that. Think about how different that is compared to most definitions, and ways of thinking about mutual respect. It focuses on self-respect, not as a condition, but as a duty. It also offers the same duty to respect others, on equal footing and ground as you respect yourself.

Bottom line, if we are asked to do something that goes against what is good for us, eff that. If we don't start with ourselves, we can never give fully to others. If your cup is not full, you cannot fill the cup of others. This comes back to positivity, as well. If my heart isn't full of positive and hopeful thoughts, how can I help someone see their world in a positive and hopeful way? You simply cannot inspire others if you're not living it in your own life.

The people I know who are successful take the time to take care of themselves, and their relationships. Whether it's a date night with their spouse, one on one time with their kids, a night out with their girlfriends, or just a hike, alone in nature. When my kids were younger, my me time was going to the gym. Now, I go see my chiropractor every two weeks, and I get a Thai massage every two weeks. It helps reduce stress, increase the strength of my immune system, and keeps my body in good shape.

Whatever it is, take care of yourself. Maybe it's going to the nail salon, or to a spin class. You have to think you are worth it to do this—so, this directly reflects on your notion of self-worth. You also have to make sure, like I mentioned before, you are making sure the people you love know their worth to you. Every year in our family, for example, my daughter and husband have their daddy-daughter Disney week. That's been their tradition for five years. Every single December, no matter what, that's their time.

People who say they only want to work, and they don't have time, or want to make time for others in their life—I think they are truly lying to themselves. They'll eventually burn-out, because they're not balancing those five pillars of their life. Self-care and self-worth almost always gets put to the side because we see it as "selfish," or not important. When I was young, for instance, I didn't value my worth. I didn't yet know the importance of building connections with myself and with others. I was truly selfish. Because I didn't value others, and I didn't value myself, I worked to work. There was no fulfillment beyond paying the bills.

You're not going to be successful without hard work. There are absolutely no shortcuts. If you think you can be successful without working hard, please return this book for a refund. We've just wasted our time together! But, seriously, hard work is necessary for all pillars of life. We just can't substitute quality time and quality relationships for the sake of hard work. You can have and do both. It just takes making that time, committing to it as you would commit to a work schedule and routine, and being aware and conscious of how you are in other people's lives, and how well you're taking care of yourself.

In a big way, mastery and Effing Simple YOU is a maturation process. Wherever you are in your life, has so much to do with your past circumstances. This self-awareness and notion of self-worth, I think, is one of the most important things we can do for ourselves, and teach our children. Unless it's nurtured, developed and respected, how can we expect to raise kids who understand that they have worth in this world? Kids must know they have value in their community and in their family. It's not something you are born with, or wake up with. It's developed from childhood, and if you didn't have that type of parenting as a child, it's something you can develop in yourself.

We say things to ourselves, about ourselves, that we would never say to a friend. We put ourselves down all the time. How many times have you looked in the mirror and thought or said to yourself, "I'm fat," or "I hate my hair," or, "I'm stupid," or "I can't do it." Bullshit! Look in the mirror and notice what you love about yourself. I love my boobs, and my butt—seriously. I love my hair. I love my smile. I love how I treat myself and others. The ability to say those things to myself didn't come naturally for me. It took practice, and it felt really weird and awkward at first. But, now I'm more comfortable with loving myself, and I find that I can love those around me more easily, too.

At the same time, know your weaknesses. I'm terrible at details. I have ideas, and when I try to get them out there, they can be a mess. But, I have people who can help me with that, so that my ideas get out there, while they worry about the details for me. Tap into your strengths as well. One of the things John Maxwell said that stood out to me was this: "If you're a 5/10 with public speaking, but an 8/10 with marketing yourself, work on that strength of marketing. Why try to develop your 5 into an 8, when you can develop your 8 into a 10?

Part of self-love is utilizing and excelling at something you're good at and something you like to do. Maybe you knit, maybe you paint, maybe you like making clothes, maybe you like collecting cars. Do it! Even in your spare time, that's part of self-love. All of this stimulates the creative part of your brain, which helps you come up with other ideas. Self-love is something that should not be put off. Just like you shouldn't make excuses for any part of your life, you shouldn't make excuses for pursuing a creative outlet. Just do it—make it—create it—be it!

I like to reward myself after I meet a goal, and I like to have that reward be related to how I value myself, and those around me. For instance, if I reach a big goal, our family will take an amazing vacation together to somewhere we never could have afforded (in time or money), before. If I do [X], I get [Y]. You can make little goals, with smaller rewards, on the way to that big reward. I see too many people say, “When I become wealthy, I will start living fabulously.” But, really, set your mindset first, and everything else follows.

For people who are working too hard on my team, I like to remind them to take care of themselves. I encourage them to take some time off or reward themselves. It’s too easy to lose balance between work, family, and friends. They are so close to the situation, and they want to succeed so badly, that they’re doing too much. When this happens, they’re usually focusing on the wrong behaviors and too many of the wrong behaviors that aren’t bringing in money. Then, it throws them completely off balance, and they stop taking care of themselves and those they love. Self-care is about finding this balance.

Being out in mother nature, shoes off, reconnecting to the earth reduces stress, and increases positivity and happiness. Nature is a natural aphrodisiac and mood elevator. Whenever you can find nature, and wherever you can find nature, go out and experience it at least three to five times a day. It can be as simple as pushing back your chair away from your computer and going outside and soaking in the fresh air and sun. It can be as easy as visiting the local park, and having a picnic in the grass. Maybe you need to drive a little bit to go out on a hike, or visit the ocean. Self-love is natural, and nature, really being in nature, is a wonderful way to tap into that.

When we are reconnecting to mother earth, we feel grounded. I go to the beach as much as I can, and literally sit there, or walk in bare feet, and just be present. I need to reconnect with nature. It just makes me happy.

Disconnect from technology. Disconnect from your screen. Disconnect from all your distractions, and get away from that. Get present in nature. Reconnect with your purpose, where you want to go, who you want to be. Nature gives us clarity. It can help us re-establish and reconnect with your purpose. Find things to do around that purpose. Uncover what's going on in your heart and soul, and make that work for you.

I've enjoyed sharing my heart and soul with you. Pursuing and expanding my purpose is the reason I wrote this book. I hope you use this effing simple advice to embrace and love YOU. Finding and committing to your purpose in life is the best way for YOU to do YOU. I believe in you!

A vision is not just a picture of what could be;

it is an appeal to our better selves,

a call to become something more.

Rosabeth Moss Kanter

Effing Simple Resources

Reading List:

Vishen Lakhiani— *The Code of the Extraordinary Mind: 10 Unconventional Laws to Redefine Your Life and Succeed On Your Own Terms*

Hal Elrod—*The Miracle Morning: The Not-So-Obvious Secret Guaranteed to Transform Your Life (Before 8AM)*

John Maxwell *Leadershift: The 11 Essential Changes Every Leader Must Embrace*

Emmanuel Ziga *The Power of One: Your Singular Journey of Purpose, Destiny & Leadership*

Gary Chapman *The 5 Love Languages: The Secret to Love that Lasts*

Downloads:

7 Steps for Daily Success *bit.ly/TV7Steps*

Objectives are Invitations *bit.ly/TVInvitations*

Effing Simple Products

Visit EfffingSimple.com to order (quantity discounts available).

	This book is an effing simple guide to help newbies and experts alike prosper and thrive in network marketing. Toni (with guest appearances from partner in crime and husband Jay Treloar) jumpstart your success with stories, strategies, and specific techniques. Recounting her 20-year and $5 million earning experience in the industry, Toni guides you through success stories, leadership strategies, and network marketing specifics.
	This journal is a companion guide to my books. If you want to have success in your life—whether that's business success, personal success, or successful relationships, it begins with taking a good hard look at your life and making the changes you need to create your life—instead of settling for the life you inherited. That's what this journal is for. It will guide you through decisions to change your life and build your business so you can get off the "hamster wheel" and truly enjoy yourself—and help others at the same time.
	Begin your day with mantras and coffee in this elegant, Effing Simple mug.

Effing Simple Daily Mantras

- It's a beautiful day.
- I am beautiful/handsome.
- I am loved.
- I am grateful.
- I am patient.
- I am successful.
- I attract abundance.
- I am walking in my purpose.
- I am a servant leader who changes lives.
- My family is blessed.
- I deserve [insert thoughts here].
- I am worthy.
- Keep it Effing Simple!

Effing Simple Thanks

Thanks for spending this time with me and committing to YOU. It's my desire to empower more people to experience Effing Simple Fulfillment. You did the right thing by purchasing this book and completing the homework. Now, go out there and You do You!!

If you'd like me to speak to your organization and get team members on board for casting the vision of their future, contact me at connect@tonivans.com.

If you'd like to interview me for your podcast, publication, or TV show, please contact my team at press@tonivans.com.

Made in the USA
Columbia, SC
15 January 2020

86807635R00085